BRAIN GAMES™

Publications International, Ltd

Contributing Writer: Holli Fort

Puzzle Constructors: Cihan Altay, Myles Callum, Kelly Clark, Jeanette Dall, Mark Danna, Harvey Estes, Josie Faulkner, Peter Grabarchuk, Serhiy Grabarchuk, Marilynn Huret, Nicole H. Lee, David Millar, Alan Olschwang, Ellen F. Pill, Ph.D., Paul Seaburn, Fraser Simpson, Shavan R. Spears, Howard Tomlinson, Kirsten Tomlinson

Additional Puzzle Editing: Fraser Simpson

Illustrators: Connie Formby, Nicole H. Lee, Anna Lender, Shavan R. Spears

Back Cover Puzzles: Howard Tomlinson

Brain Games is a trademark of Publications International, Ltd.

Louis Weber, CEO
Publications International, Ltd.
7373 North Cicero Avenue
Lincolnwood, Illinois 60712

Permission is never granted for commercial purposes.

ISBN-13: 978-1-4127-1450-1
ISBN-10: 1-4127-1450-8

Manufactured in U.S.A.

8 7 6 5 4 3 2 1

CONTENTS

Start your mental workout with these nice and easy puzzles.

Stretch your mind with these more challenging puzzles.

Increase the intensity with this brain-enhancing mix of puzzles.

Take your brain workout to the next level with these demanding puzzles.

Go the distance with these puzzles, the most challenging of the bunch.

BRAIN FITNESS

Your mind is your most important asset—more important than your house, your bank account, and your stock portfolio. You insure your house and work hard to pad your bank account. But what can you do to sharpen your mind and protect it from decline? With the baby boomer generation getting on in years, an increasing number of people are asking this question. Modern-day science provides a clear answer: Protect your mind by protecting your brain. To understand this relationship further, we turn to cutting-edge research.

Protect and Enhance Your Brainpower

Modern-day neuroscience has established that our brain is a far more plastic organ than was previously thought. In the past it was believed that an adult brain can only lose nerve cells (neurons) and cannot acquire new ones. Today we know that new neurons—and new connections between neurons—continue to develop throughout our lives, even well into advanced age. This process is called *neuroplasticity*. Thanks to recent scientific discoveries, we also know that we can harness the powers of neuroplasticity in protecting and even enhancing our minds at every stage of life—including our advanced years.

How can we harness neuroplasticity to help protect and enhance our mental powers? Recent scientific research demonstrates that the brain responds to mental stimulation much like muscles respond to physical exercise. In other words, you

have to give your brain a workout. The more vigorous and diverse your mental life—and the more you welcome mental challenges—the more you will stimulate the growth of new neurons and new connections between them. Furthermore, the *nature* of your mental activities influences *where* in the brain this growth takes place. The brain is a very complex organ with different parts in charge of different mental functions. Thus, different cognitive challenges exercise different components of the brain.

How do we know this? We've learned this by experiments created from real-life circumstances and *neuroimaging*, the high-resolution technologies that allow scientists to study brain structure and function with amazing precision. Some say that these technologies have done for our understanding of the brain what the invention of the telescope has done for our understanding of the planetary systems. Thanks to these technologies, particularly MRI (magnetic resonance imaging), we know that certain parts of the brain exhibit an increased size in those who use these parts of the brain more than most people. For example, researchers found that hippocampi, the parts of the brain critical for spatial memory, were larger than usual in London cab drivers who have to navigate and remember complex routes in a huge city. Studies revealed that the so-called Heschl's gyrus, a part of the temporal lobe of the brain involved in processing music, is larger in professional musicians than in musically untrained people. And the angular gyrus, the part of the brain involved in language, proved to be larger in bilingual individuals than in those who speak only one language.

What is particularly important is that the size of the effect—the extent to which the part of the brain was enlarged—was

directly related to the *amount of time* each person spent in the activities that rely on the part of the brain in question. For instance, the hippocampal size was directly related to the number of years the cab driver spent on the job, and the size of Heschl's gyrus was associated with the amount of time a musician devoted to practicing a musical instrument. This shows that cognitive activity directly influences the structures of the brain by stimulating the effects of neuroplasticity in these structures, since the enlargement of brain regions implies a greater than usual number of cells or connections between them. The impact of cognitive activity on the brain can be great enough to result in an actual increase in its size! Indeed, different parts of the brain benefit directly from certain activities, and the effect can be quite specific.

Diversify Your Mental Workout

It is also true that any more or less complex cognitive function—be it memory, attention, perception, decision making, or problem solving—relies on a whole network of brain regions rather than on a single region. Therefore, any relatively complex mental challenge will engage more than one part of the brain, yet no single mental activity will engage the whole brain.

This is why the diversity of your mental life is key to your overall brain health. The more vigorous and varied your cognitive challenges, the more efficiently and effectively they'll protect your mind from decline. To return to the workout analogy: Imagine a physical gym. No single exercise machine will make you physically fit. Instead, you need a balanced and diverse workout regime.

You have probably always assumed that crossword puzzles and sudoku are good for you, and they are. But your cognitive workout will benefit more from a greater variety of exercises, particularly if these exercises have been selected with some knowledge of how the brain works.

The puzzle selection for *Brain Games*™ has been guided by these considerations—with knowledge of the brain and the roles played by its different parts in the overall orchestra of your mental life. We aimed to assemble as wide a range of puzzles as possible, in order to offer the brain a full workout.

There is no single magic pill to protect or enhance your mind, but vigorous, regular, and diverse mental activity is the closest thing to it. Research indicates that people engaged in mental activities as a result of their education and vocation are less likely to develop dementia as they age. In fact, many of these people demonstrate impressive mental alertness well into their eighties and nineties.

What's more, the pill does not have to be bitter. You can engage in activities that are both good for your brain *and* fun. Different kinds of puzzles engage different aspects of your mind, and you can assemble them all into a

cognitive workout regime. Variety is the name of the game—that's the whole idea! In any single cognitive workout session, have fun by mixing puzzles of different kinds. This book offers you enough puzzle variety to make this possible.

Welcome challenging puzzles, instead of feeling intimidated by them. Never give up! To be effective as a mental workout, the puzzles should not be too easy or too difficult. An overly easy puzzle will not stimulate your brain, just as a leisurely walk in the park is not an efficient way to condition your heart. You need mental exertion. On the other hand, an overly difficult puzzle will just frustrate and discourage you from moving forward. So it is important to find the "challenge zone" that is appropriate for you. This may vary from person to person and from puzzle to puzzle. Here too, the gym analogy applies. Different people will benefit most from different exercise machines and from different levels of resistance and weights.

With this in mind, we have tried to offer a range of difficulty for every puzzle type. Try different puzzles to find the starting level appropriate to you. And before you know it, your puzzle-cracking ability will improve, your confidence will grow, and this will be a source of reassurance, satisfaction, and even pride.

Have Fun While Stretching Your Mind

The important thing is to have fun while doing something good for you. Puzzles can be engaging, absorbing, and even addictive. An increasing number of people make regular physical exercise part of their daily routines and miss it when circumstances prevent them from exercising. These habitual gym-goers know that strenuous effort is something to look forward to, not to avoid. Similarly, you will strengthen your mental muscle by actively challenging it. Don't put the puzzle book down when the solution is not immediately apparent. By testing your mind you will discover the joy of a particular kind of accomplishment: watching your mental powers grow. You must have the feeling of mental effort and exertion in order to exercise your brain.

This brings us to the next issue. While all puzzles are good for you, the degree of their effectiveness as brain conditioners is not the same. Some puzzles only test your knowledge of facts. Such puzzles may be enjoyable and useful to a degree, but they're not as useful in conditioning your brain as the puzzles that require you to transform and manipulate information or do something with it by logic, multistep inference, mental rotation, planning, and so on. The latter puzzles are more likely to give you the feeling of mental exertion, of "stretching your mind," and they are also better for your brain health. You can use this feeling as a useful, though inexact, assessment of a puzzle's effectiveness as a brain conditioner.

Try to select puzzles in a way that complements, rather than duplicates, your job-related activities. If your profession involves dealing with words (e.g., an English teacher), try to emphasize spatial puzzles. If you are an engineer dealing with diagrams, focus on verbal puzzles. If your job is relatively devoid of mental challenges of any kind, mix several types of puzzles in equal proportions.

Cognitive decline frequently sets in with aging. It often affects certain kinds of memory and certain aspects of attention and decision making. So it is particularly important to introduce cognitive exercise into your lifestyle as you age to counteract any possible cognitive decline. But cognitive exercise is also important for the young and the middle-aged. We live in a world that depends increasingly on the brain more than on the brawn. It is important to be sharp in order to get ahead in your career and to remain at the top of your game.

How frequently should you exercise your mind and for how long? Think in terms of an ongoing lifestyle change and not just a short-term commitment. Regularity is key, perhaps a few times a week for 30 to 45 minutes at a time. We've tried to make this easier by offering a whole series of *Brain Games*™ books. You can carry these puzzle books—your "cognitive workout gym"—in your briefcase, backpack, or shopping bag. Our puzzles are intended to be fun, so feel free to fit them into your lifestyle in a way that enhances rather than disrupts it. Research shows that even a relatively brief regimen of vigorous cognitive activity often produces perceptible and lasting effects. But as with physical exercise, the results are best when cognitive exercise becomes a lifelong habit.

To help you gauge your progress, we have included two self-assessment questionnaires: one near the beginning of the book and one near the end. The questionnaires will guide you in rating your various cognitive abilities and any change that you may experience as a result of do-

ing puzzles. Try to be as objective as possible when you fill out the questionnaires. Improving your cognitive skills in real-life situations is the most important practical outcome of exercising your mind, and you are in the best position to note such improvement and to decide whether or not it has taken place.

Now that you're aware of the great mental workout that awaits you in this book, we hope that you'll approach these puzzles with a sense of fun. If you have always been a puzzle fan, we offer a great rationale for indulging your passion! You have not been wasting your time by cracking challenging puzzles—far from it; you have been training and improving your mind.

So, whether you are a new or seasoned puzzle-solver, enjoy your brain workout and get smarter as you go!

ASSESS YOUR BRAIN

You are about to do something very smart: Embark on a set of exercises to improve your mind. But before you begin, take a moment to fill out this self-assessment questionnaire. It is for your own benefit, so you know how your brain works before you challenge it with *Brain Games*™ puzzles. Then you will be able to track any changes in your mental performance and discover the ways in which you have improved.

The questions below are designed to test your skills in the areas of memory, problem solving, creative thinking, attention, language, and more. Please reflect on each question, and rate your responses on a 5-point scale, where 5 equals "excellent" and 1 equals "very poor." Then tally up your scores and check out the categories at the bottom of the next page to learn how to sharpen your brain.

1. After attending a party where you meet 5 to 10 new and interesting people, how skilled are you at remembering their names the next day?

1   2   3   4   5

2. When going to a new place for the first time, how confident are you that you'll remember the directions? If you often get lost, deduct a point from your score.

1   2   3   4   5

3. How capable are you at planning your daily activities? Do you make a schedule and stick to it, or do you find yourself scrambling to get things done each day?

1   2   3   4   5

4. Consider this scenario: You have a full day of meetings and events at work. Then an important client calls at the last minute to reschedule an appointment. How good are you at juggling your schedule to accommodate this unanticipated change?

1   2   3   4   5

5. How well do you remember news stories? Can you remember in good detail at least three stories you read in the paper, heard on the news, or saw on television in the past 24 hours?

1   2   3   4   5

6. Consider this scenario: You're working on an assignment with a tight deadline, but your brother keeps calling to ask you questions about the vacation you're taking together next month. Rate your ability to stay on task without getting distracted.

1   2   3   4   5

7. When you're doing several different things at once—multitasking—do you feel that you are giving the appropriate amount of attention to each task? Say you're baking a cake, sorting the laundry, and having a phone conversation with your best friend. Can you have a good chat without burning the cake or accidentally putting a red sock in with your whites?

1   2   3   4   5

8. When you're trying to describe something, are you good at expressing yourself clearly and succinctly? Deduct points if you sometimes have trouble finding exactly the right word.

1   2   3   4   5

9. How good is your ability to do simple math in your head without using a calculator?

1   2   3   4   5

10. Consider this scenario: You're planning an anniversary party for your sister and are responsible for all the details, including food, entertainment, invitations, and venue. How good are you at this type of event planning? (If you could track down everything and throw a perfect party, give yourself a 5. If you're less organized and would end up forgetting to hire a caterer, give yourself a 1.)

1   2   3   4   5

10–25 Points:
Are You Ready to Make a Change?

Remember, it's never too late to improve your brain health! A great way to start is to work puzzles on a regular basis, and you've taken the first step by picking up this book. Choose a different type of puzzle each day, or do a variety of them to help strengthen memory, focus attention, and improve logic and problem solving.

26–40 Points:
Building Your Mental Muscle

You're no mental slouch, but there's always room to sharpen your mind! Choose puzzles that will challenge you, especially the types of puzzles you might not like as much or would normally avoid. Remember, doing a puzzle can be the mental equivalent of doing lunges or squats: While they might not be your first choice of activity, you'll definitely like the results!

41–50 Points:
View from the Top

Congratulations! You're keeping your brain in tip-top shape. To maintain this level of mental fitness, keep challenging yourself by working puzzles every day. Like the rest of the body's muscles, your mental strength can decline if you don't use it. So choose to keep your brain strong and active. You're at the summit—now you just have to stay to enjoy the view!

WARM UP YOUR MIND

A-MAZE-ing Race

PLANNING **SPATIAL REASONING**

Can you get from Alaska to Zanzibar? Actually, we'll settle for A to Z.

Answer on page 171.

11

Crossed Words

Write each word below in the grid. They will only fit one way.

3 Letters
CAR
CAT

4 Letters
BABY
BELL
BOAT
FISH
PLAY
ROSE
SHOE
SNOW

5 Letters
HORSE
HOUSE

6 Letters
FARMER
FATHER
FLOWER
MOTHER

8 Letters
AIRPLANE

Soft to Hard

You can change the word SOFT to the word HARD in just 5 steps. Solve the clues, changing only one letter on each line. Do not change the order of the letters.

SOFT

Prepare the laundry _____

Painful _____

Apple center _____

Phone wire _____

King or queen _____

HARD

Answers on page 171.

Starburst

Continue to fill in the alphabet moving clockwise around the wheel. Place 1 letter in each space. When the alphabet is complete, unscramble the 5 letters at the 5 points of the star to form a common 5-letter word.

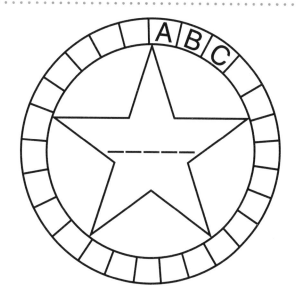

Sudoku

Use deductive logic to complete the grid so that each row, each column, and each 3×3 box contains the numbers 1 through 9 in some order. The solution is unique.

3		9		8	5	1	2	
6				2	9	7		5
	7		1					
		5			2		9	
	2		6		3		7	
	6		8			3		
					6		3	
2		6	9	3				7
	8	3	2	1		5		9

Answers on page 171.

What's the Problem?

In the following equation, the letters A, B, and C represent whole numbers. Using the information given, solve the final equation.

If $A \times B = 6$

and $B \times C = 15$

and $A \times C = 10$,

what is $A + B + C$?

Maze-I Tov!

That's what we'll say if you can find your way out of this one!

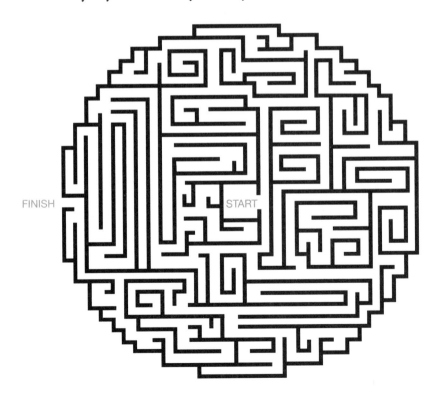

FINISH   START

Answers on page 171.

Types of Cakes

LANGUAGE   ATTENTION   VISUAL SEARCH

Every word listed is contained within the box of letters below. The words can be found in a straight line horizontally, vertically, or diagonally. They may read either backward or forward.

ALMOND

ANGEL FOOD

APPLESAUCE

BANANA

BIRTHDAY

BUNDT

CARROT

CHEESE

CHERRY

CHIFFON

CHOCOLATE

COCONUT

COFFEE

DATE

```
C O C O N U T O R R A C B P W
H H T J Y E L L O W E W A E B
I D O I Z E G D U F X Y N A I
F W R C U B T N N I S I A R R
F P H M O R D N O M L A N L T
O R U I O L F M A P L E A D H
N A P H T D A T E P S C N E D
L L S T Y E P T E E Y U O V A
R I I R R O E Q E C B A M I Y
E N D C U Z Z H F A Q S E L E
G E E N Z M C M F N M E L S N
N C D E G N A R O M U L P F O
I I O Y R R E H C C D P S O H
G P W E D D I N G Z H P D O H
Z S N D O O F L E G N A C D Y
```

DEVIL'S FOOD

FRUIT

FUDGE

GINGER

HONEY

ICE CREAM

LAYER

LEMON

MAPLE

MOCHA

MUD

ORANGE

PEAR

PECAN

PLUM

POUND

PRALINE

RAISIN

RUM

SHORT

SPICE

SPONGE

TEA

UPSIDE-DOWN

WEDDING

WHITE

YELLOW

Answers on page 171.

Autumn Delight

Across

1. Rainy day infield cover
5. Part of Batman's getup
9. Jazz musician ___ Calloway
12. Margarine
13. Patron saint of Norway
14. Apple pie ___ mode
15. Natural downside of Autumn
18. "Born in the ___," Bruce Springsteen song
19. Lipton product
20. Sibling's daughter
21. Prepare a salad, perhaps
23. Madam's counterpart
24. Sad news item, briefly
26. Forever, seemingly
27. Health club feature
30. Autumn sporting events
34. Ardent devotee
35. Sort
36. Salsa and French onion, e.g.
37. High or low card
38. Crucifix
40. Like a dishonest deal
43. "Hey, that hurt!"
44. Acquired
47. In Autumn, students look forward to this ... or do they?
50. Lyricist Gershwin
51. Fireplace fodder
52. Data, informally
53. Snoop around
54. Shorten a sentence, maybe
55. "Hey buddy ... over here"

Down

1. Vegetarian staple
2. "Sad to say ..."
3. Kinship
4. Vote seeker, briefly
5. Ice cream holders
6. Pond scum
7. Chum
8. Time for a soiree
9. Hangout for bats
10. Actor Guinness
11. Pedestal
16. "___ a girl!"
17. Ventilate
22. Giant Mel of Cooperstown
23. Our sun
24. "Keep ___ the Grass"
25. Feathery scarf
26. BPOE member
27. Tiny amounts
28. Vim
29. Beast of burden
31. Eco-friendly transport
32. Ginger ___ (soft drink)
33. Botheration
37. Commercials

38. Perch
39. Barn bird
40. Little cut
41. Munich Mister
42. Not home
43. Bear or Berra
45. Dimwits
46. Horse's gait
48. Brick carrier
49. Puppy sound

Answers on page 172.

Loop de Loop

Fill in the empty cells of the grid so that each black star is surrounded by the digits 1 through 8 with no repeats.

3	7		★			8	6
1	★	4			7	★	4
5	2		★			3	5
8	★					★	7
7	1		★			1	4
★			1	2	7		

Where ARE They?

Ignoring spaces and punctuation, how many occurrences of the consecutive letters A-R-E can you find in the paragraph below? For example, the phrase "lunar eclipse" contains the word "are" hidden inside it: lunAR Eclipse.

On a dare, Carey called Marie, a regular at his favorite bar, expecting to get her cell phone. Marie scares easily so she compared his number to her speed-dial list and didn't answer. Carey ate a pear and decided to visit Bar, ex-wife number two, but car engine trouble forced him to take a cab and share fare with a fair-haired lass named Clair, who told him he didn't have a prayer with her. Bar doesn't care for Carey so she had current boyfriend Gary blare a red horn to scare Carey away.

Trivia on the Brain
Neurons last for a whole lifetime. They are some of the oldest cells in the human body.

Answers on page 172.

Who's There?

Cryptograms are messages in substitution code. Break the code to read the message. For example, THE SMART CAT might become FVO QWGDF JGF if F is substituted for T, V for H, O for E, and so on.

"YVHH, MR M STHHVO BQV YCGKN

KDLWVC, YQX OMO XGD TKEYVC

BQV JQGKV?"

—PTLVE BQDCWVC

Really Sum-thing

Fill in each empty cell of the grid with a number 1 through 9. The sum (addition) of the numbers in each row must be the value to the right of that row of the grid, and the sum of each column must be the value below that column of the grid. The numbers in each diagonal must add up to the values in the upper and lower right corners.

9

7			**19**
8	1		**13**
			13

20 12 13 14

Answers on page 172.

One Cut

With 1 straight line, divide the shape to the left into 2 pieces of equal area.

An Arm and a Leg

LANGUAGE   PLANNING

Change just one letter on each line to go from the top word to the bottom word. Do not change the order of the letters. You must have a word at each step.

1. ARM

————————
————————
————————
————————

LEG

2. SOLE

————————
————————
————————

CARP

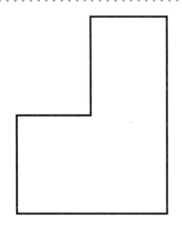

3. PLAY

————————
————————
————————

STOP

4. VEAL

————————
————————
————————

BEEF

Answers on page 172.

Mirror, Mirror

There's no trick here, only a challenge: Draw the mirror image of these familiar objects. You may find it harder than you think!

Flock of Fs

This picture contains a flock of things beginning with the letter **F**. We count 9 things. How many can you find?

Answers on page 172.

Spin the Dials

Imagine that each of the dials below can spin. Turn each dial to form a 6-letter word reading straight across the middle of the 3 dials.

Trees in Words

Each of the 7 words below contains the name of a tree. The trees' names may read either forward or backward.

1. Beefsteaks

2. Eyewitness

3. Harmlessly

4. Red-letter

5. Sleepiness

6. Soothsayer

7. Spendthrift

Answers on page 172.

Number Climber

Help the mountaineer reach the summit by filling the boulders (circles) with numbers. Each boulder is the sum (the total when added) of the 2 numbers in the boulders that support it. For example: 2 + 3 = 5. If a total is 10 or more, only write the second digit. For example: 7 + 6 = 13; write 3.

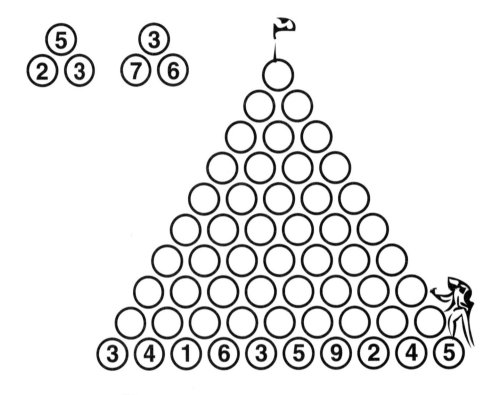

Trivia on the Brain

The human cerebral cortex has an area of about 2.5 square feet, has 25 billion neurons, is interconnected by more than 100,000 kilometers of axons, and receives 300 trillion synapses. The cerebral cortex is about as thick as a tongue depressor and grows thicker as knowledge is gained and used.

Answer on page 173.

Layer by Layer

Thirteen sheets of paper—each the same size and shape—were piled on a table. Number the sheets 1 through 13, with 1 as the top sheet and 13 as the bottom sheet.

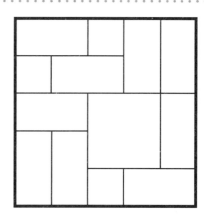

Geometric Shapes

Divide the grid into smaller geometric shapes by drawing straight lines either following the grid lines or diagonally across the cells. Each formed shape must have exactly one symbol of the same shape inside it.

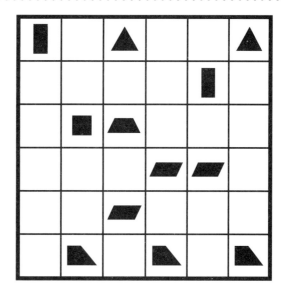

Answers on page 173.

Name Calling

Decipher the encoded words in the quips below using the numbers and letters on the phone pad. Remember that each number can stand for any of three or four possible letters.

1	2 ABC	3 DEF
4 GHI	5 JKL	6 MNO
7 PQRS	8 TUV	9 WXYZ
	0	

1. A virtuoso is a musician with very high 6-6-7-2-5 standards.

2. 8-4-7-8-8-3 is its own punishment.

3. The 4-4-7-2-3-3-3 is the highest form of animal life.

4. Help Wanted: Dynamite factory. Must be willing to 8-7-2-8-3-5.

5. Remember, paper is always 7-8-7-6-6-4-3-7 at the perforations.

Rhyme Time

Answer each clue below with a pair of rhyming words. The numbers that follow each clue indicate how many letters are in each word. For example, "Cookware taken straight from the oven" (3, 3) would be "hot pot."

1. Became overheated (3, 3) _____

2. Rudely ignore Chicago baseballer (3, 4) _____

3. Sluggish river current (4, 4) _____

4. College housing application (4, 4) _____

5. Fissure movement (4, 5) _____

6. Arrive at sandy expanse (5, 5) _____

7. Majestic raptor (5, 5) _____

8. More elegant cruise ship (5, 5) _____

9. Reading room with tracked-in muck (5, 5) _____

10. Unpleasant surprise from a market decline (5, 5) _____

Answers on page 173.

Count the Dots

How many dots do you count in the picture below?

Ho-Hum Advice

Cryptograms are messages in substitution code. Break the code to read the message. For example, THE SMART CAT might become FVO QWGDF JGF if F is substituted for T, V for H, O for E, and so on.

"UJPC   HC   RFQVO,   MHCL   BFQR."

—KFVPKO   APKKHBB

Answers on page 173.

Let's Get Away From It All

Across

1. Bio and chem, e.g.
5. British nobleman
9. Man of morals?
14. Sighed words
15. Medical picture
16. Courageous
17. Early television sitcom
20. Other than
21. Jealousy
22. Before, poetically
23. Infamous Roman emperor
25. Mt. Rushmore's st.
27. Sleep state, for short
30. Merit
32. Busybodies
36. Medical school subj.
38. New corp. hires
40. Editor's mark
41. "Get lost!"
44. Dangerous bacteria
45. Scarlett's plantation
46. Skin cream additive
47. Like a high-pitched scream
49. Spinnaker, for one
51. Sunday lect.
52. Commoner
54. Shawl or stole
56. Salty expanse
59. "_____ to please!"
61. Enchants

65. "Come on, stay a while!"
68. Japanese, perhaps
69. Campus club, commonly
70. Simple melody
71. Leases
72. _____ Fifth Avenue
73. Observes

Down

1. Mall attraction
2. General Mills cereal
3. Apple computer product
4. Lucky number, for some
5. Highway egress
6. Sculpture or dance
7. $10/hour, say
8. French silk center
9. Temporary suspension
10. Important time period
11. Use a piggy bank
12. Above
13. Pierre's pop
18. Blunted sword
19. Some briefs, briefly
24. Planet's path
26. Australian eucalyptus eater
27. Rants and raves
28. Methuselah's father
29. Of prime importance
31. Grannies
33. Tough exams

34. Tea type
35. Beef source
37. Bloom associated with Holland
39. Barn floor covering
42. A great deal
43. Salon offerings
48. Bit of foliage
50. Cowardly Lion portrayer
53. Punches
55. Formal agreements

56. Play the lead
57. Abate
58. Similar (to)
60. Pianist Hess
62. Lecher
63. Lion's locks
64. Fr. holy women
66. Chow down
67. Acorn's future identity

Answers on page 173.

Rock Around the Record Maze

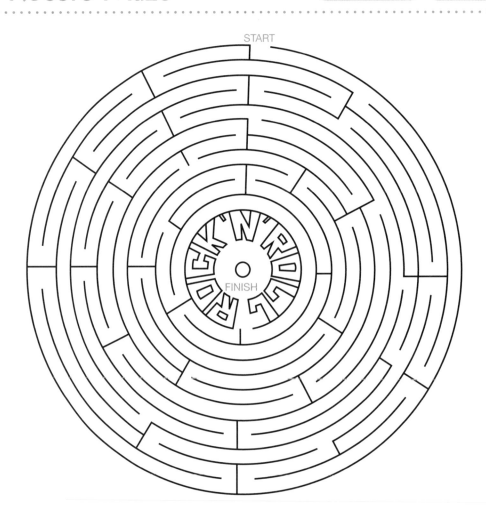

START

FINISH

Trivia on the Brain

The Greek philosopher Aristotle believed that the heart, not the brain, was the seat of mental processes.

Answer on page 173.

It Has a Ring

Every word listed is contained within the group of letters below. The words can be found in a straight line horizontally, vertically, or diagonally. They may read either backward or forward.

BATHTUB

BOXER

BRIDE

CHIMES

CIRCUS

DOORBELL

GONG

GROOM

JEWEL BOX

JEWELER

JINGLE BELLS

SATURN

SLEIGH BELLS

TELEPHONE

WEDDING

XYLOPHONE

```
        S G N O G X I
        L O O N Y E B
        L I L L D R A
        E P O I G E T
        B P R D N U H
      S H B G O E R T H
      O G N H O C L U B
     N R I P A R R I B T O
     E O D E N T B L U R C A R
   M O D L L U S E M I H C E S K
   M E E T S P E L L B O L U N G
   W T E J I N G L E B E L L S O
   X O B L E W E J R W B O X E R
             A W E
              J
```

Answers on page 173.

31

Sudoku

Use deductive logic to complete the grid so that each row, each column, and each 3×3 box contains the numbers 1 through 9 in some order. The solution is unique.

2					7		4	5
		5	2			7	1	
		6	5				2	9
			6					4
5	1	4	3		9	2	6	7
9					2			
6	4				1	5		
	5	2			4	1		
3	8		7					2

Initial Impression

We hope you don't come up short trying to figure out what these famous abbreviations stand for!

1. B&O, the railroad

2. CARE, the foreign-aid organization

3. ECG, at a hospital

4. GMT

5. ISBN, to a librarian

6. LED, in electronics

7. NASA

8. RSVP, on an invitation

9. SAM, the military weapon

10. SWAK, on a love letter

Answers on page 174.

Pathway

Draw a single closed path passing through each empty cell of the grid exactly once and moving only horizontally and vertically.

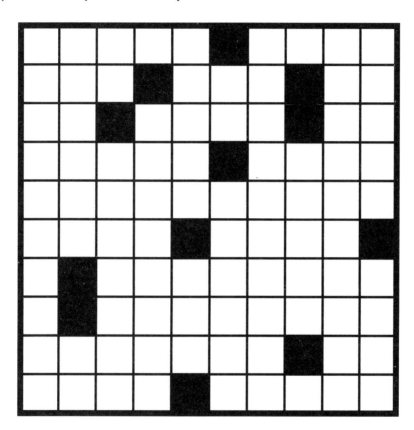

Trivia on the Brain

After early childhood and until puberty, synapses in the human neocortex are lost at a rate of 100,000 synapses per second.

Answer on page 174.

Donut Maze

Nothing eases the Monday-morning blues like a donut. If you can find your way through this maze, you'll be on your way to a great week!

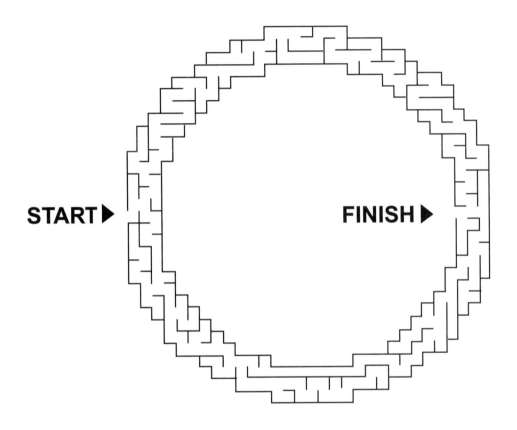

Time Will Tell

Can you "read" the phrase below?

WAITC

Answers on page 174.

Geometric Shapes

SPATIAL REASONING   LOGIC

Divide the grid into smaller geometric shapes by drawing straight lines either following the grid lines or diagonally across the cells. Each formed shape must have exactly one symbol of the same shape inside it.

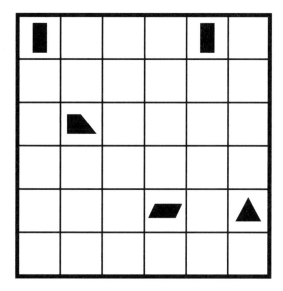

Cities and States

LANGUAGE   GENERAL KNOWLEDGE

Without scrambling any of the original letters, spell the names of six United States cities or states by adding one letter to each word below. Letters may be inserted anywhere in the words.

FARO

INDIAN

MINE

SALE

SETTLE

TEAS

Answers on page 174.

Warm Up Your Mind

Traffic Light

LANGUAGE **GENERAL KNOWLEDGE**

Across

1. Shingle words
6. Leaning Tower's locale
10. Atlas pages
14. When repeated, a Yale cheer
15. Baldwin of "Prelude to a Kiss"
16. Suffix with switch
17. Shaq's game: sl.
18. Juror, in theory
19. Comparable
20. 1971 Richard Thomas film
23. Keep them about you
24. Peter, Paul, and Mary
25. Hall of Famer, e.g.
28. Midler of "The Rose"
30. Not for kids
31. German auto
32. Zimbalist drama, with "The"
35. Way in "The Wizard of Oz"
39. NBC weekend comedy
40. Rubik creation
41. "Biography" network
42. Clumps of grass
44. Highly valued
45. Andre of the courts
48. Hammerhead
49. Dr. Seuss book
55. In case
56. "Damn Yankees" girl
57. Bent out of shape
58. Mayberry jailbird
59. Contest for two

60. Forbidden acts
61. Ending with silver or soft
62. Flower supporter
63. Church areas

Down

1. E.g., e.g.
2. Half of Hamlet's question
3. Unit of laundry
4. "No trouble to report"
5. Enter
6. Mamas' mates
7. "Why should ___ you?"
8. Appear
9. Type of word puzzle
10. Nasty sort
11. Actor Alan
12. Decimal dot
13. "Yesterday" and "Tomorrow"
21. From Jan. 1 to now
22. Informer
25. Produces eggs
26. Forbidden fruit site
27. Coastal bird
28. City outskirts, briefly
29. Singer Adams
31. Go to the edge of
32. Winkler role, with "the"
33. Expressed, as a welcome
34. Picked out of a lineup
36. "The Bank Dick" actor
37. Tolstoy's Anna

36

38. Bit of precipitation
42. Fly in the tropics
43. PT boats are in it
44. Soup legume
45. Radiant
46. Actress Garbo
47. Norse race

48. Biblical poem
50. Joint inflammation
51. Euphoria
52. First name in fairy tales
53. Stick ___ in the water
54. Tough spot

Answers on page 174.

Buy It Online

Every word listed is contained within the box of letters below. The words can be found in a straight line horizontally, vertically, or diagonally. They may read either backward or forward.

ANTIQUES

ART SUPPLIES

BEAD KITS

CARDS

CELL PHONES

CHIMES

COMFORTERS

DESIGNER CLOTHES

DISCS

DISHES

DOLLS

EASELS

ELECTRONICS

FLOWERS

```
C  H  I  M  E  S  N  E  N  I  L  Y  E  A  D
O  A  G  E  M  S  S  E  M  A  G  L  P  N  E
M  A  R  T  Q  P  N  W  Y  X  E  H  R  T  S
F  R  B  D  Z  O  L  E  G  C  A  A  I  I  I
O  T  E  Y  S  R  T  S  T  N  Y  Z  N  Q  G
R  S  A  R  F  T  N  R  D  S  S  S  T  U  N
T  U  D  X  E  I  O  B  S  R  E  I  S  E  E
E  P  K  S  M  N  A  J  L  E  N  K  G  S  R
R  P  I  A  I  G  W  D  Z  W  O  S  L  T  C
S  L  T  C  S  G  R  Z  O  O  H  H  A  L  L
X  I  S  P  O  O  N  S  B  L  P  A  S  I  O
V  E  S  L  O  O  T  D  L  F  L  T  S  U  T
M  S  C  S  I  D  E  A  S  E  L  S  E  Q  H
D  I  S  H  E  S  P  O  S  T  E  R  S  Y  E
W  S  A  B  U  T  E  L  E  S  C  O  P  E  S
```

GAMES

GEMS

GLASSES

HANDBAGS

HATS

LAYETTES

LINENS

NUTS

POSTERS

PRINTS

QUILTS

SHOES

SKIS

SPOONS

SPORTING GOODS

TELESCOPES

TOOLS

TUBAS

USED BOOKS

VITAMINS

YARN

Answers on page 174.

Rhyme Time

Answer each clue below with a pair of rhyming words. The numbers that follow each clue indicate how many letters are in each word. For example, "Cookware taken straight from the oven" (3, 3) would be "hot pot."

1. Order to appear before the boss (3, 2) _____
2. Police chief (3, 3) _____
3. Overweight belfry resident (3, 3) _____
4. "Dinner, immediately!" (4, 3) _____
5. Previous year's performers (4, 4) _____
6. Despots on the Red Planet (4, 5) _____
7. Incorrect flip-flop (5, 5) _____
8. Small horse's pals (5, 7) _____

Try a Little Love

Change just one letter on each line to go from the top word to the bottom word. Do not change the order of the letters. You must have a word at each step.

HATE

_____

_____

_____

LOVE

Answers on pages 174–175.

A Little Mix-up [ATTENTION] [LANGUAGE] [LOGIC]

We're sure you're familiar with these 6 items, but their names have gotten mixed up into anagrams. Unscramble them and put the correct numbers and letters together.

1. WOK FRIERS _____

2. CLOAK EPISODE _____

3. RAIN PLEA _____

4. NOSY CAR _____

5. GREY SCOOP _____

6. COP SPIEL _____

A.

B.

C.

D.

E.

F.

Answers on page 175.

No Shoes, No Shirt, No Service

LOGIC CREATIVE THINKING

To protest other restaurants' "No shoes, no shirt, no service" policy, the sign on the door of the Hippy Dippy Vegetarian Restaurant reads: "Bare feet only." One Monday, 20 people showed up for dinner—7 wearing socks, 5 wearing shoes, and 4 wearing both. How many people were allowed in?

Layer by Layer

SPATIAL REASONING   CREATIVE THINKING

Twelve sheets of paper—each the same size and shape—were piled on a table. Number the sheets 1 through 12, with 1 as the top sheet and 12 as the bottom sheet.

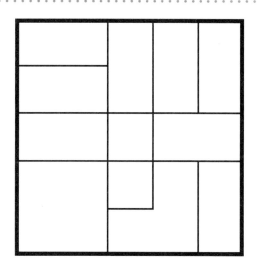

Trivia on the Brain

The brain is about the size of a cantaloupe and is wrinkled like a walnut. Some even say it feels like a ripe avocado.

Answers on page 175.

Dog Dishes

The biggest dog gets the biggest dish. From the relative size of the dishes below, can you tell which dog is the biggest?

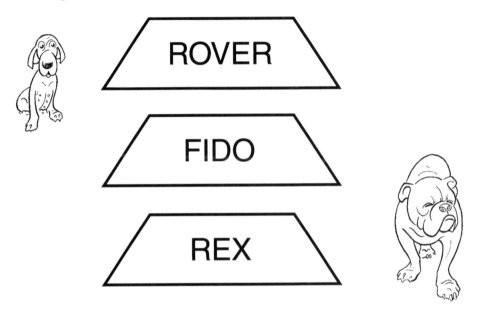

Trivia on the Brain

The left side of the brain controls the right side of the body and is the control center for rational and logical thinking. The right side of the brain controls the left side of the body and is responsible for creative and intuitive thinking.

Answer on page 175.

Bevy of Bs

We count 11 things in this picture that begin with the letter **B.** How many can you find?

Answers on page 175.

Totally Cube-ular!

Which of the shapes below can be folded to form the cube in the center? There may be more than one.

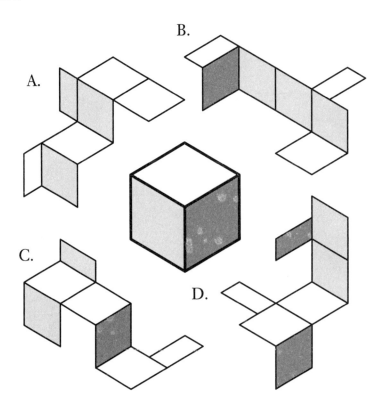

Trivia on the Brain
The human brain is approximately 75% water but is capable of having more ideas than the number of atoms in the known universe!

Answers on page 175.

The Ten Spot

LANGUAGE **ATTENTION** **VISUAL SEARCH**

Ignoring spaces and punctuation, how many occurrences of the consecutive letters T-E-N can you find in the paragraph below? For example, the phrase "white noise" has the word "ten" hidden inside it: whi<u>TE N</u>oise.

Ted Tennyson the Third often attended a tent dance with fifteen tense gents pretending to entertain nineteen tender lasses with short attention spans. In a tender moment, enthralled by the music, Tennyson asked the DJ to play the hits of Ten Years After. Tennyson and his pal Pat endured eight entire songs before a spat ended the night.

Shooting Star

LANGUAGE **ATTENTION**

Continue to fill in the alphabet moving clockwise around the wheel. Put one letter in every third space until you fill in the whole wheel. Use all 26 letters of the alphabet. Then unscramble the 5 letters at the 5 points of the star to form a common 5-letter word.

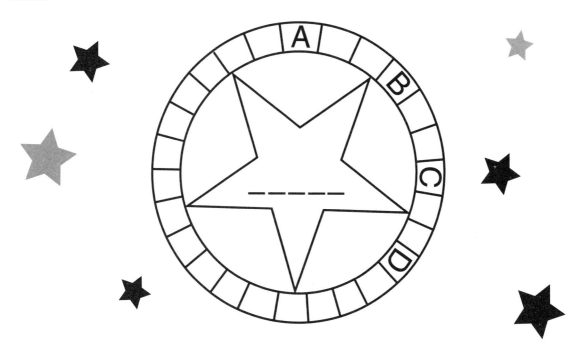

Answers on page 175.

I Owe, I Owe...

Change just one letter on each line to go from WORK to CASH. Do not change the order of the letters. You must have a word at each step.

WORK

_____

_____

_____

_____

CASH

Name Calling

Decipher the encoded words in the quips below using the numbers and letters on the phone pad. Remember that each number can stand for any of three or four possible letters.

1. So easy to use a child can do it. Child sold 7-3-7-2-7-2-8-3-5-9.

2. Common sense 2-4-6'-8.

3. A king's castle is 4-4-7 4-6-6-3.

4. Length, width, height, and cost are the four 3-4-6-3-6-7-4-6-6-7.

1	2 ABC	3 DEF
4 GHI	5 JKL	6 MNO
7 PQRS	8 TUV	9 WXYZ
	0	

Answers on page 175.

And a 1, and a 2...

Fill in each empty cell of the grid with a number 1 through 9. The sum (addition) of the numbers in each row must be the value to the right of that row of the grid, and the sum of each column must be the value below that column of the grid. The numbers in each diagonal must add up to the values in the upper and lower right corners.

					20
	4	4	3	1	20
3	2	6	7		25
9		1	1	6	25
8		9	2	5	33
2		1		8	17
30	26	21	16	27	21

Pretty Fontsy!

Our favorite new inventor, Larry Letterman, has just been inspired by his name to create an alphabet soup using different fonts for the letters. He gave this presentation to a big soup company, but in a careless moment he put one letter in twice, in the same shade, font, and size. He hates to repeat himself. Can you find the letter?

m r h X t o d e G w L ℓ c B
H J f i n Q m a z n o z m V
e L o r ◦ k u ⌠ F y w k p g
N z D ◘ W v x t a T u X ℐ c
y b H v R k g I c j E t p U

Answers on page 175.

Spinning Gray into Gold

Change just one letter on each line to go from the top word to the bottom word. Do not change the order of the letters. You must have a word at each step.

1. GRAY
_____
_____
_____
_____
GOLD

2. BLUE
_____
_____
_____
GRAY

3. BLACK
_____
_____
_____
_____
GREEN

4. ROSE
_____
_____
JADE

5. TEAL
_____
_____
_____
LIME

Number Theory

Cryptograms are messages in substitution code. Break the code to read the message. For example, THE SMART CAT might become FVO QWGDF JGF if F is substituted for T, V for H, O for E, and so on.

HVJDJ   LDJ   HVDJJ   PCTSZ   GI   FJGFYJ—HVGZJ

MVG   XLT   XGWTH   LTS   HVGZJ   MVG   XLT'H.

Answers on page 175.

The State of Things

Every word listed is contained within the box of letters below. The words can be found horizontally, vertically, or diagonally and may read either backward or forward.

ALABAMA

ALASKA

ARIZONA

COLORADO

CONNECTICUT

DELAWARE

FLORIDA

GEORGIA

HAWAII

IDAHO

ILLINOIS

INDIANA

KANSAS

KENTUCKY

LOUISIANA

MAINE

MICHIGAN

MISSISSIPPI

MISSOURI

MONTANA

NEVADA

NEW YORK

OHIO

OREGON

TEXAS

UTAH

VERMONT

VIRGINIA

WYOMING

```
F O T O S S C K A A S R H Y I H
A G I U A I R O N L M A K A E V
I H E X C O O A L I A C S N T E
O N E O Y I I N S O U B I N L U
E T D W R S T S I T R A A A A R
N E E I I G I C N L M A D M M K
I N N U A S I E E G L I D O A W
H A O V S N K A N N R I N O T E
A L M I I N A I D U N T V E R S
T L P I O R M F O E A O V A A T
H P A G C O G S L N L E C R E A
I A E S Y H S I A O R A I I D O
A R W W K I I M N M R Z W A H T
O O B A M A E G O I O I V A C O
N T E N I T P N A N A E D H R I
L I P P I I T A A N N I N A S E
```

Answers on page 176.

In the Drink

LANGUAGE   **GENERAL KNOWLEDGE**

Across

1. Backslid
7. Piece for a niche
11. All tix. sold notice
14. Rally
15. von Bismarck
16. Beach acquisition
17. Ariel, for one
18. Max the satirist
20. Relative of Cod or Ann
22. Drillmaster's order
23. "___ the hills and far away"
24. Delivery from the mound
26. Sandy's expressions
28. Religious devotion
29. Priest: Fr.
33. Less than a min.
34. Eater of bamboo
35. Play a guitar
36. Dreaded
38. Gratify
39. ___ boat to China
40. Daily record
43. Grandfather of King Saul
44. Count on
45. Inasmuch as
46. Whirlpool
47. Palette user
49. English cathedral city
50. Cultivator
53. Softened a blow
57. Expression of amusement
59. Above the timberline
60. Writer McEwan
61. Grand in scope
62. Shop or store: Sp.
63. Roman X
64. Assay
65. After this

Down

1. Whip
2. Harp: Ital.
3. Freighter's destination
4. "Grand Canyon" and "Peer Gynt"
5. Chemical salt
6. Whitetail
7. Snow racer
8. Utah native
9. Regular date
10. Rich layer cake
11. Greek mall
12. What some teams hear
13. "The joke's ___"
19. Scold
21. "It's ___ to tell…"
25. "Let's call ___ day"
26. "___ as I'm concerned"
27. Della or Pee Wee
28. Cushion
30. Scene of British victory in 1777
31. Used surface transportation
32. Corundum
34. Seat for a congregant

50

35. Foxlike
37. Kansas City players
38. Before: pref.
40. Half of MIV
41. Scrutinize
42. Start of a play
45. Make lines
46. Person who marries on the run
48. Convened once more

49. J. R.'s mother
50. Foolish person
51. Dies ___: Lat.
52. A Redgrave
54. Plaster support
55. Within: pref.
56. "Daffy" or "Dizzy"
58. Fleur de ___

Answers on page 176.

Legion of Ls

ATTENTION   **VISUAL SEARCH**

We count 12 things in this picture that begin with the letter **L**. How many can you find?

Answers on page 176.

Family Ties

Some words related to the family are hidden in this grid. To spell a word, start at any letter and move from letter to letter by traveling to any adjacent letter—up, down, across, or diagonally—but do not come back to a letter you've used previously in that word. Can you find 10 family words?

```
A  P  O  C  S
P  A  U  S  I
F  R  T  N  M
O  H  E  O  I
M  M  S  C  E
```

Sudoku

Use deductive logic to complete the grid so that each row, each column, and each 3×3 box contains the numbers 1 through 9 in some order. The solution is unique.

	1	9		7				6
		2				7	8	5
				2			9	
8			6		2		3	
	2		4		7		5	
	5		1		8			2
	3			6				
1	8	5				6		
9				8		2	4	

Answers on page 176.

Countdown

LANGUAGE   **LOGIC**

Cryptograms are messages in substitution code. Break the code to read the message. For example, THE SMART CAT might become FVO QWGDF JGF if F is substituted for T, V for H, O for E, and so on. The same code is used in each quote below.

"ZJNX LXOBF, MSVXC CNX GNISBN FSV

UANLQ; PI DNBF LXOBF, LX JVXHBNH."

—CJSRLU KNIINBUSX

"ZJNX LXOBF, MSVXC ISVB; ZJNX DNBF

LXOBF, UZNLB."

—RLBQ CZLPX

Job Search

ATTENTION   **LANGUAGE**   **VISUAL SEARCH**

O S W R S
N F A I T
O M R T L
A D E O C
I R L A V

Some names of jobs are hidden in this grid. To spell a word, start at any letter and move from letter to letter by traveling to any adjacent letter—up, down, across, or diagonally—but do not come back to a letter you've used previously in that word. Can you find 12 jobs?

Answers on page 176.

ABCD

Place the letter A, B, C, or D in each square of the grid. The tables above and to the left of the grid indicate how many times each letter appears in that column or row. No letter can be horizontally or vertically adjacent to itself.

A	3	0	2	0	2	2
B	1	2	0	2	2	2
C	1	2	2	2	1	1
D	1	2	2	2	1	1

A	B	C	D						
0	2	2	2						
3	0	2	1						
0	3	0	3						
2	0	2	2						
1	3	1	1						
3	1	2	0						

Rhyme Time

Answer each clue below with a pair of rhyming words. The numbers that follow each clue indicate how many letters are in each word. For example, "Cookware taken straight from the oven" (3, 3) would be "hot pot."

1. Substantial swine (3, 3) _____
2. Purchase pastry dessert (3, 3) _____
3. Look for mountaintop (4, 4) _____
4. High-pitched dentist's tool (4, 5) _____
5. Frighten grizzly (5, 4) _____
6. Pony Express route (4, 5) _____
7. Malicious monarch (4, 5) _____
8. Too-cool young mare (6, 5) _____
9. Polite request for cheddar (6, 6) _____
10. Larger ship worker (6, 6) _____

Answers on page 176.

Reach the "Sum"mit

COMPUTATION   **LOGIC**

Help the mountaineer reach the summit by filling the boulders (circles) with numbers. Each boulder is the sum (the total when added) of the 2 numbers in the boulders that support it. For example: 2 + 3 = 5. If a total is 10 or more, only write the second digit. For example: 7 + 6 = 13; write 3.

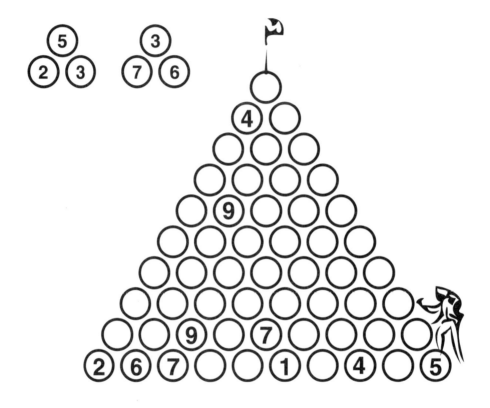

Trivia on the Brain

The brain of a grasshopper has approximately 16,000 neurons. The human brain contains 100 billion neurons.

Answer on page 176.

Mirror, Mirror

There's no trick here, only a challenge: Draw the mirror image of these familiar objects. You may find it harder than you think!

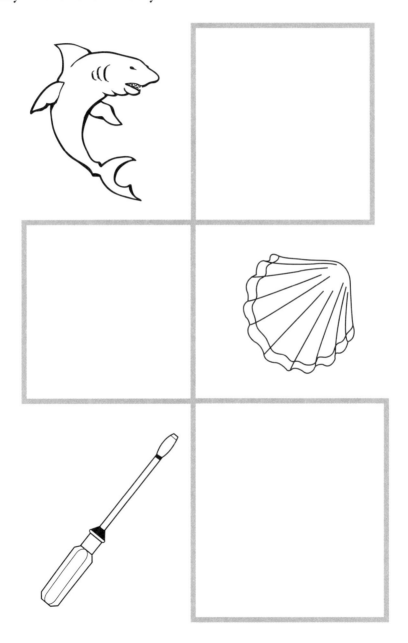

Funny Farm

ATTENTION   VISUAL SEARCH

This is by far the strangest farm in the country. We count 7 wrong things in this picture. How many can you find?

Trivia on the Brain

At 1,400 g, the human brain is smaller than an elephant's brain (4,780 g) but bigger than a monkey's brain (95 g)! By comparison, a dog's brain weighs about 72 g, and a cat's brain weighs about 30 g.

Answers on page 176.

The Times Tables are Turned!

Fill in each empty cell of the grid with a number 1 through 9. The product (multiplication) of the numbers in each row must be the value to the right of that row of the grid, and the product of each column must be the value below that column of the grid. By multiplying the numbers in each diagonal, you should arrive at the values in the upper and lower right corners.

75

	3		**30**
	5	4	**80**
3			**6**

24 15 40 20

Picnic Puzzle

Sally was preparing a picnic lunch for her hungry family. First, she covered the square table with a red-and-white checkerboard tablecloth that had 64 squares on its top surface. Then she put a pitcher of lemonade in each of 2 diagonal corner squares of the tablecloth. She had a plate of 31 hoagie sandwiches, each one big enough to cover 2 adjacent squares of the tablecloth. Sally wanted to put the hoagies on the tablecloth and cover the remaining 62 squares with no hoagies overlapping, none hanging over the edge of the table, and none standing on end. Was she able to figure out a way to do it before her hungry family showed up to eat them?

Answers on page 177.

Training Exercise

Run your train through the maze, entering and exiting with the arrows. Remember: You can't back up, and you can't jump track at the crossovers—you must go straight through them.

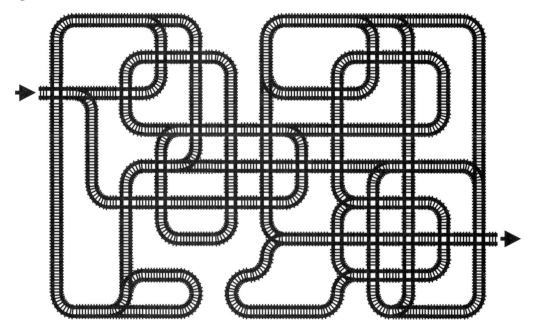

It's a Song

Can you "read" the phrase below?

N

O

O

M

D

A

B

Answers on page 177.

Count the Dots

How many dots do you count in the picture below?

Sound of Music

Determine the missing letter in this logical progression.

D, R, M, F, ___, L, T, D

Answers on page 177.

Sudoku

Use deductive logic to complete the grid so that each row, each column, and each 3×3 box contains the numbers 1 through 9 in some order. The solution is unique.

6	4			3	8	9		
			2	9			6	
		5	1					
5	6			4	3	8		2
9		8	6	5			3	4
					9	3		
	7			6	2			
		6	7	1			4	9

East to West

Change just one letter on each line to go from the top word to the bottom word. Do not change the order of the letters. You must have a word at each step.

1. EAST

_____

_____

   WEST

2. BALL

_____

_____

   GAME

3. DOGS

_____

_____

   WOOF

4. RAGS

_____

_____

   RICH

5. WILD

_____

_____

_____

   TAME

6. NAIL

_____

_____

_____

   FILE

7. CATS

_____

_____

   DOGS

Answers on page 177.

Coffee Break   ATTENTION   LANGUAGE   VISUAL SEARCH

Every word listed is contained within the box of letters below. The words can be found in a straight line horizontally, vertically, or diagonally. They may read either backward or forward.

ACIDITY

ARABICA

AROMA

BAGS

BEANS

BLEND

BRAZIL

BREW

BRIGHTNESS

CAFFEINE

CANISTER

CAPPUCCINO

COFFEE PRESS

CREAM

DARK

```
C O F F E E P R E S S W T D B
A A S R O V A L F Y T X S E L
F R P G V L M O H C I R A T E
F S T P U W A V X S W N O A N
E W A A U M E T S K S S R N D
I E A H M C R E T R S S H I G
N E W T C U C Y L E K G C E J
E T K B E O S I R P I A N F R
G E E Z R R M P N K M B E F L
R N N P O E S V R O M P R A I
I E Y X B E W A R N I I F C Z
N R A G U S D A Z A L R E E A
D R E T S I N A C V K D Z D R
E T S A T S S E N T H G I R B
R X A R A B I C A C I D I T Y
```

FRENCH ROAST   MUGS   SUMATRA

GRINDER   PERKS   SWEETENER

ICED   RICH   TASTE

KENYA   ROBUSTA   WATER

KONA   SKIM MILK

LATTE   STRONG

MOCHA   SUGAR

DARK

DECAFFEINATED

DRIP

DRY PROCESS

ESPRESSO

FLAVORS

FOAM

Answers on page 177.

Get a Move On

Across

1. Drinking spree
5. Repeat
9. Automobile type
14. Overhang
15. Pal
16. Grassy plain
17. Sonny's ex
18. Part
19. Lubricated
20. Way of life, in the army
23. Automobile
24. Bread soaked in liquid
25. Fit ___ fiddle
27. Ancient Greek promenade
31. Fight against
36. WWII battle site
38. Killer whale
40. Nancy Drew creator
41. Children's game
44. "...partridge in ___ tree"
45. Withered
46. "___ the night before..."
47. Minnow
49. Drunkards
51. "You ___ There," hosted by Cronkite
52. Sticky substance
54. Showery mo.
56. Old-fashioned
64. City in upstate New York

65. Periods
66. Roman "fiddler"
67. River mouth
68. Pinball slip-up
69. Cafeteria item
70. Ford flop
71. Only
72. Nick Charles's dog

Down

1. Georgia or Cal
2. Hawaiian isle
3. Outbid, in bridge
4. ___ firma
5. Yellowish brown
6. Sever
7. Hawaiian dance
8. Portents
9. Laggard
10. Lamb pen name
11. Spanish surrealist
12. Dill herb
13. Realm of dreams
21. Lots of mos.
22. One of the dwarfs
25. "___ as the eye can see"
26. Excavate in layers
28. Pull
29. Table scraps
30. Pains
32. Butcher's stock

33. Hot pans for cold sheets
34. Close at hand
35. Succinct
37. Norse king
39. Sol or space beginning
42. Initial
43. Permit
48. Oui's opposite
50. College ent. exam
53. "Waiting for Lefty" playwright

55. Nina companion
56. Drained
57. Conger and moray
58. Despise
59. Threesome
60. Town ___ meeting
61. This: Sp.
62. Part of Q.E.D.: Lat.
63. Substitute for 32-Down
64. Lyric poem

Answers on page 177.

Count the Shapes

Start seeing things from a different angle! Count the number of triangles of all sizes in the diagram below.

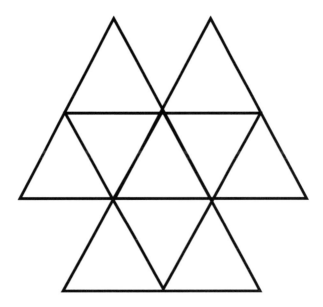

Trivia on the Brain

Myelin, the fatty material that wraps around some nerve fibers to insulate them, makes the brain more efficient and allows messages to travel faster. Without myelin, the human brain would have to be 10 times bigger than it is now, and we would have to eat 10 times as much to maintain it.

Answer on page 178.

Word Jigsaw

Fit the pieces into the frame to form common, uncapitalized words reading across and down crossword-style. There's no need to rotate the pieces; they'll fit as shown, with each piece used exactly once.

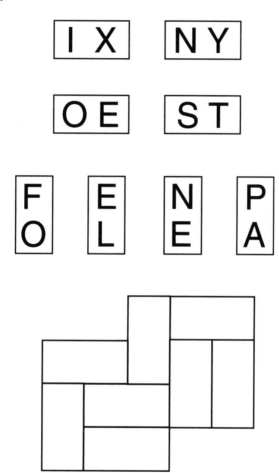

Trivia on the Brain
The word "cerebellum" comes from the Latin words meaning "little brain."

Answer on page 178.

How Many?

How many words can you find here that answer the question "How many?" We found 15. To spell a word, start at any letter and move from letter to letter by traveling to any adjacent letter—up, down, across, or diagonally—but do not come back to a letter you've used previously in that word.

```
H  T  W  S  E
Y  R  E  L  C
T  N  E  V  O
H  G  I  N  R
U  D  O  Z  E
```

Three-Letter Anagrams

LANGUAGE

Fill in the blanks in each sentence below with words that are anagrams (rearrangements) of one another.

1. She _____ a trophy and _____ she is happy.

2. Dad gave me a _____ on my shoulder and a _____ on my head.

3. The queen sipped her _____ and _____ a scone.

4. We drove the _____ over an _____-shaped bridge.

5. The _____ gave birth to a _____ lamb.

Answers on page 178.

68

ABCD

Place the letter A, B, C, or D in each square of the grid. The tables above and to the left of the grid indicate how many times each letter appears in that column or row. No letter can be horizontally or vertically adjacent to itself.

		A	1	2	1	3	0	2
		B	2	2	2	0	2	1
		C	3	0	1	2	2	1
A	B	C	D	0	2	2	1	2	2
3	1	1	1						
2	0	2	2						D
0	3	1	2						
3	0	2	1						
0	3	1	2						
1	2	2	1					D	

Prvrbs

Can you figure out these proverbs without their vowels?

STTCHNTMSVSNN

BTTRLTTHNNVR

LLSWLLTHTNDSWLL

Answers on page 178.

A Single Letter

What single letter, when placed in front of any one of these five words, spells a new word?

___URGE

___ROSE

___IRATE

___LACE

___HONE

It's All Relative

A cryptogram is a message in substitution code. Break the code to read the message. For example, THE SMART CAT might become FVO QWDGF JGF if F is substituted for T, V for H, O for E, and so on.

"XJNE V CVE OFQO XFQJ V IMNQQZ HFMA

LGM VE JGSM, FQ ONNCO AFBN V CFESQN. TSQ

ANQ JFC OFQ GE V JGQ OQGUN LGM

V CFESQN—VEP FQ'O AGEHNM QJVE VE JGSM.

QJVQ'O MNAVQFUFQZ."

—VATNMQ NFEOQNFE

Answers on page 178.

Dawn to Dusk

LANGUAGE   PLANNING

Change just one letter on each line to go from the top word to the bottom word. Do not change the order of the letters. You must have a word at each step.

1. DAWN

_____

_____

_____

_____

   DUSK

2. JUMP

_____

_____

_____

_____

   LAND

3. BOOT

_____

_____

_____

   KICK

4. BOAT

_____

_____

_____

   FISH

5. WAVE

_____

_____

_____

   SURF

6. KISS

_____

_____

_____

   LOVE

Related Women

CREATIVE THINKING   LOGIC

Sally's sister Jane has no children. Mary is Jane's niece, but she is not Sally's niece. What relation is Mary to Sally?

Answers on page 178.

Sudoku

Use deductive logic to complete the grid so that each row, each column, and each 3×3 box contains the numbers 1 through 9 in some order. The solution is unique.

		8			9	4		7
4		5	1	6				
	1							6
6	9	2	7	8		3		4
	5						7	
3		4		9	5	2	8	1
5							6	
				7	4	8		3
9		7	2			1		

Making Music

Can you "read" the phrase below?

L
O
A
D
S
O
N
G
S

Answers on page 178.

72

The But-Not Game

The object of the "But-Not" Game is to uncover the element common to each statement.

Carol likes felines but not cats.

Carol likes halibut but not flounder.

Carol likes palaces but not castles.

So . . . what does Carol like?

Game Time

Can you "read" the phrase below?

INNING

INNING

INNING

INNING

INNING

INNING

I   N   N   I   N   G

Trivia on the Brain

The weight of the human brain triples during the first year of life, going from 300 grams to 900 grams.

Answers on page 178.

BOOST YOUR BRAINPOWER LEVEL 3

Tessellated Floor

PLANNING SPATIAL REASONING

Rearrange the seven pieces to form the mosaic shape. Pieces can be rotated but not overlapped or mirrored.

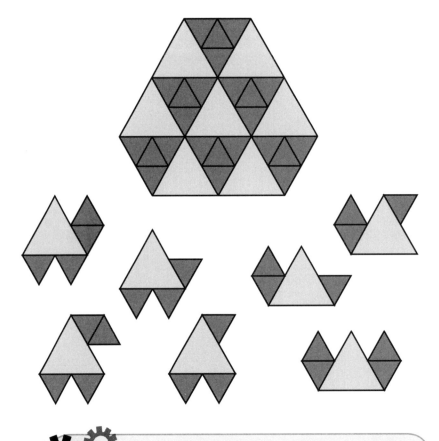

Trivia on the Brain
The part of the brain called the cerebellum controls muscle movement, balance, and coordination.

Answer on page 178.

What's Missing?

Find the one letter that, when placed in each of the five spaces below, completes a common phrase.

___ AT ___ H   AS   ___ AT ___ H   ___ AN

Three Ways

Without using a ruler, determine which of these lines is the longest.

Trivia on the Brain

Eating "brain foods"—foods rich in vitamin E, beta-carotene, and vitamin C—may help lower your risk of Alzheimer's disease.

Answers on page 178.

Cruising Along

LANGUAGE   ATTENTION   VISUAL SEARCH

Every word listed is contained within the box of letters below. The words can be found in a straight line horizontally, vertically, or diagonally. They may read either backward or forward.

ACTIVITIES

BINGO

BUFFETS

CABIN

CAPTAIN

CASINO

CHEF

CLASSES

COUNSELOR

DANCING

DECK

DRINKS

GAMES

GIFTS

GOLF

GYM

HIGH TEA

ISLES

KARAOKE

LECTURES

LIBRARY

LOUNGES

```
S K C A N S E S S A L C K Y T
K C A C T I V I T I E S A H H
N E P R O M E N A D E W R C S
I D T M X G E S E M A G A N T
R R A A Z O N S H G N B O U E
D A I S S I N I R I Z A K L F
Y W N S B T I I B U G C E O F
R E W A W S F M S O N H Y O U
A T C G L F I I Y A I E T P B
R S M E A L S Z G G C F G E S
B D S T C R O L E S N U O C A
I S S K M O O R E T A T S Y U
L E C T U R E S V I D E O S N
L O U N G E S O L A R I U M A
R E T A E H T O U R S A L O N
```

LUNCH

MASSAGE

MEALS

NURSE

POOL

PROMENADE

ROCK CLIMBING

SALON

SAUNA

SNACKS

SOLARIUM

STAFF

STATEROOM

STEWARD

THEATER

TOURS

VIDEOS

YOGA

Answers on page 179.

900 Total

Place each of the numbers 1 through 9 in the squares below to create three 3-digit numbers that add up to 900. There are several possible answers. Can you come up with at least two?

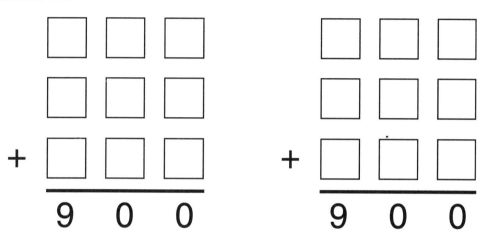

For Your Eyes Only

Using your eyes only: Are the 2 black stars larger, smaller, or the same size as the white stars?

Answers on page 179.

High Times

Across

1. Constellation's second brightest star
5. Exponent
10. For men only
14. Sacred image
15. Early adding machines
16. Arizona native
17. Biblical structure
20. Pain
21. Of gulls
22. Challenge
23. Goes over a book again
24. Scrawny fellows
27. Moronic
28. Hearten
29. Actor and photographer Lollobrigida
30. Ashen
33. Noted disaster movie, with "The"
37. Wall, State, et al
38. "Mildred Pierce" author
39. Stradivarius's teacher
40. Suit piece
41. Repast
42. Testy
46. Casserole ingredient
47. Antiaircraft fire
48. Produce
52. Famous campanile
54. Labor
55. Sample
56. Asian princess
57. Male offspring
58. Go in
59. "Auld Lang ___"

Down

1. Pieces' partner
2. Alpine answer
3. Rule follower
4. Come before
5. Rough handlers
6. Beyond chubby
7. "Star ___"
8. Environmental: pref.
9. '50s TV show, with "The"
10. Extra
11. Leg bone
12. Make corrections
13. Strong winds
18. Old-time catapult
19. Biting remark
23. Quarrel
24. Hardens
25. Solidify
26. Edges that aren't hemmed
27. Finger
29. Grind one's teeth
30. Stole
31. Pot starter
32. Black: Fr.
34. Emulate Kwan
35. Tap
36. Napoleon and Hirohito

40. Squad's target
41. "Shosha" author
42. Bulb units
43. "Gesundheit" elicitor
44. Yarn bundle
45. Becomes tiresome

46. French income
48. Main point
49. Removed
50. Miss. neighbor
51. Toledo's lake
53. A Bobbsey twin

Answers on page 179.

Mrs. Smith's Daughters

Jane, Anna, Kate, and Sarah are Mrs. Smith's 4 daughters. Each daughter has a different hair color (black, blond, brown, or red) and a different eye color (blue, brown, green, or hazel). Using the information given, try to determine not only each daughter's hair and eye color but also whether she is one, two, three, or four years old.

1. The girl with black hair is younger than Sarah.

2. Of Jane and Anna, one has brown hair and the other has brown eyes, but neither is the oldest or youngest.

3. Kate does not have hazel eyes.

4. The blond is younger than the girl with green eyes but older than Anna.

		JANE	ANNA	KATE	SARAH	HAIR BLACK	HAIR BLOND	HAIR BROWN	HAIR RED	EYES BLUE	EYES BROWN	EYES GREEN	EYES HAZEL
	4 YEARS OLD												
	3 YEARS OLD												
	2 YEARS OLD												
	1 YEAR OLD												
EYES	BLUE												
EYES	BROWN												
EYES	GREEN												
EYES	HAZEL												
HAIR	BLACK												
HAIR	BLOND												
HAIR	BROWN												
HAIR	RED												

Answers on page 179.

Remember Me?, Part I

Study these pictures for 2 minutes, then turn the page to take a quiz.

Remember Me?, Part 2

(Don't look at this page until you've finished studying the items on page 81!)

Circle the names of the objects you saw on the preceding page.

PIANO

UMBRELLA

FLAG

WINDMILL

BANANAS

GRATER

DOUGHNUTS

BOTTLE

HARMONICA

CAMERA

ANCHOR

VIOLIN

PINEAPPLE

COMPASS

TEAPOT

PUMPKIN

Answers on page 179.

Amazing Bout with a Trout

START

FINISH

Cryptoquote

A cryptogram is a message in substitution code. Break the code to read the message. For example, THE SMART CAT might become FVO QWGDF JGF if F is substituted for T, V for H, O for E, and so on. Hint: N equals G.

"BFS JDD QHFW KNNM RZ HZK

EJMYKS—JZP OJSGA SAJS EJMYKS."

—UJWY SOJRZ

Answers on page 179.

Crowd of Cs

We count 13 things in this picture that begin with the letter **C.** How many can you find?

Sweet Dreams

LANGUAGE   PLANNING

Change just one letter on each line to go from the top word to the bottom word. Do not change the order of the letters. You must have a word at each step.

SLEEP

_____

_____

_____

_____

_____

DREAM

Answers on page 179.

Sudoku

Use deductive logic to complete the grid so that each row, each column, and each 3×3 box contains the numbers 1 through 9 in some order. The solution is unique.

		1	3		7			
8								
			6	7	4	2		
	1		8			6		9
	4						5	
3		8	5				4	
	8	7	4	1				
								3
	9		7		8			

Bird Wisdom

Cryptograms are messages in substitution code. Break the code to read the message. For example, THE SMART CAT might become FVO QWGDF JGF if F is substituted for T, V for H, O for E, and so on. The code is the same for each cryptogram below.

1. F LNIV NM XFMV NG EAISX SEA

    NM SXJ LZGX.

2. LNIVG AO F OJFSXJI OKABH SADJSXJI.

3. SXJ JFIKR LNIV DJSG SXJ EAIC.

Answers on page 180.

Altered States

Every word or phrase listed is contained within the box of letters below. Words can be found in a straight line diagonally. They may read either backward or forward. As an added challenge, see if you can figure out the theme of this puzzle.

A HEN WHIMPERS

A HUT

BANKS ARE

COOL ROAD

GYM I OWN

HA! I DO!

I'M ACHING

I MEAN

IN NAVY PLANES

IT IS WAVERING

LAND ARMY

LEWD AREA

LOOK! A HAM!

NOMINATES

NOT A MAN

OLD FAIR

SO LAUNCH A RIOT

TAXES

TEEN SENSE

WE MIX ONCE

WINS COINS

WORN KEY

```
L E V E R S Y Y O W H O N S E
O A F T E H E M I L N A O E S
E I N X T K C N A O D L I S A
N I A D N E S O M H A F I D S
A T N R A C E I O U A T A R O
N A O N O R N N N L I K E I G
E W G I A A M C S S R P O E R
R R N N T V H Y W E M O C O A
N S A E I A Y A N I N N A E L
A W S S R H V P H A O S R D M
T O O I K E C W L X M A E N F
T U O I R N N A I A D A A H E
N T H I M E A M M W N E T A M
E O N A H Y E B E I M E F O A
U G S A S W G L T I A T S E N
```

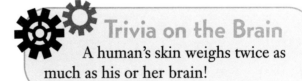

Trivia on the Brain
A human's skin weighs twice as much as his or her brain!

Answers on page 180.

Rhyme Time

Answer each clue below with a pair of rhyming words. The numbers that follow each clue indicate how many letters are in each word. For example, "Cookware taken straight from the oven" (3, 3) would be "hot pot."

1. Order to the miners (4, 3) _____
2. Cruel college employee (4, 4) _____
3. Ten-story shopping center (4, 4) _____
4. Plumber's duty (4, 4) _____
5. Essential household task (4, 5) _____
6. Neutral colored brimless hat (4, 5) _____
7. Ancient Egyptian card game (5, 5) _____
8. She gets better rest (6, 7) _____
9. Zoo employee who works for less (7, 6) _____
10. TV series finale (4, 9) _____

Triangle Cut

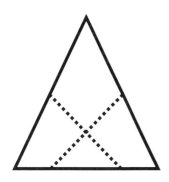

If this triangle is cut along the dotted lines, can the four sections be arranged to form a perfect square? No need to use a protractor to solve this puzzle. We think you can do it with just your eyes.

Answers on page 180.

ABCD

Place the letter A, B, C, or D in each square of the grid. The tables above and to the left of the grid indicate how many times each letter appears in that column or row. No letter can be horizontally or vertically adjacent to itself.

				2	2	1	1	1	2
			A	2	2	1	1	1	2
			B	2	0	2	2	2	1
			C	2	1	1	0	3	2
A	B	C	D	0	3	2	3	0	1
2	1	1	2						
2	1	2	1						
1	2	2	1					A	
1	2	2	1						
2	1	2	1	A					
1	2	0	3						

Two Rules

Cryptograms are messages in substitution code. Break the code to read the message. For example, THE SMART CAT might be FVO QWGDF JGF if F is substituted for T, V for H, O for E, and so on.

HNMFM TFM HIG FPQMK WGF PQHCJTHM

KPAAMKK CO QCWM: OMSMF HMQQ

MSMFLHNCOY LGP EOGI.

Answers on page 180.

Corporate Office Maze

START

FINISH

Answer on page 180.

Cube It!

Fill in this crossword with numbers instead of letters. Use the clues to determine which of the numbers 1 through 9 belongs in each square. No zeros are used.

Across

1. A perfect cube that is a palindrome (reads the same backward as it does forward)
4. A multiple of 9
5. Its digits add up to 16
7. Its middle digit is the sum of its two outside digits

Down

1. A multiple of 17
2. A palindrome
3. A number of the form ABAB
6. Its first digit is twice its last digit

Count the Shapes

How many rectangles of all sizes are formed by the lines of this diagram?

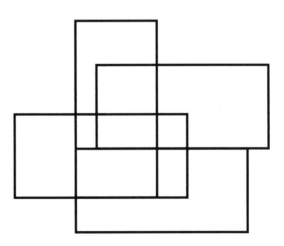

Answers on page 180.

Myriad of Ms

Within this picture we count 14 things that begin with the letter **M.** How many can you find?

Star

There are 10 triangles in the star below: A-C-D, D-E-G, G-H-J, F-H-I, B-C-F, B-D-J, A-G-I, B-E-H, C-E-I, and A-F-J. Add 5 new lines to the star to create a total of 35 triangles.

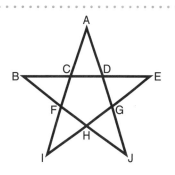

Answers on page 181.

Boost Your Brainpower

Treed

Across

1. Foot in verse
5. Glades
10. Murray and West
14. Bar follower
15. "Middlemarch" author
16. Jerez jar
17. Handle, for Horace
18. Lobo
20. Prescribed amounts
22. Balzac's "Le ___ Goriot"
23. Woods's prop
24. Pert lass
26. Gallaudet beneficiary
28. Unmarried male
32. Pumice
36. Seraglios
37. Chemical ending
38. Inclination
39. Muralist José Maria
40. Gambled
43. Drat!
44. Athenian demagogue
46. Cicero's "Where?"
47. Rational
48. Minor Persian despot
50. Bridged
52. Dutch export
54. Conserv.
55. So. state
58. Part of a geom. sign-off
60. Old magistrates

64. Exponents in higher math
67. Fast time
68. "Jeopardy!" host, to friends
69. Caravansary
70. Freeway portion
71. Created
72. Time periods
73. Fillip

Down

1. Hussein's former land
2. Japanese aborigine
3. "Wild Horse ___" (Grey)
4. Mercantile subsidiary
5. Assigned
6. Samuel's counselor
7. Flaccid
8. Like oak leaves
9. Metrical measures
10. Cut grass
11. Thanks ___
12. She: Fr.
13. Ump's call
19. Respond
21. "___ Kiss": Rodin
25. Morrison, of literature
27. Old Wimbledon rival
28. Autumn pears
29. Miss St. Johns
30. Editor's mark
31. Like some gems
33. Stately

34. Jejune
35. Used an abacus
41. Zaragoza's river
42. Diacritical mark
45. Consumer advocate
49. Congregation
51. Norm.
53. San ___, CA
55. Hoax

56. Manilow's girl of song
57. Matured
59. N.Y. type way
61. Spare
62. Sicilian resort
63. Child or ladder
65. Bunyan's tool
66. Cover with graffiti

Answers on page 181.

Boost Your Brainpower

A-Dissection

PLANNING **SPATIAL REASONING**

Can you divide this shape into 3 equal parts? You can only "cut" along the lines of the grid. Shapes may be mirrored.

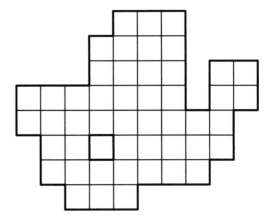

Card Positions

LOGIC

The 4 playing cards below have been chosen from each of the 4 suits in a deck of cards. There is an ace, a king, a queen, and a jack. Assuming that the cards are facing you, determine the rank and suit of each card.

1. The ace is farther to the right than the spade.

2. The diamond is farther to the left than the queen, and the club is farther to the right than the queen.

3. The heart is farther to the left than the jack, and the spade is farther to the right than the jack.

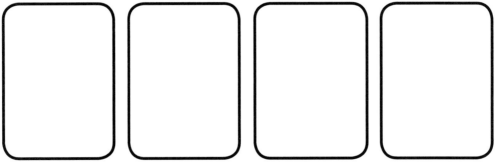

Answers on page 181.

Turnabout Maze

Trivia on the Brain
Fetal neurons multiply at a rate of 250,000 neurons per minute during early pregnancy.

Answer on page 181.

Count the Dots

How many dots do you count in the picture below?

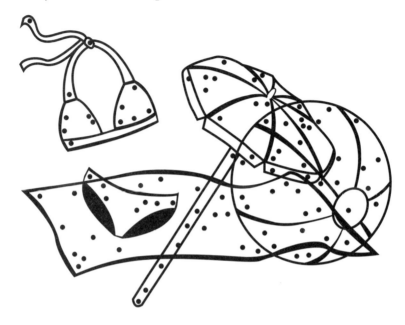

Chess Squares

How many squares are formed by the horizontal and vertical lines of a standard chessboard?

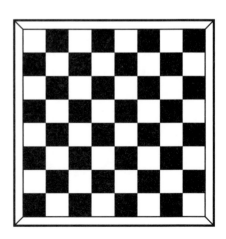

Answers on page 181.

Sudoku

LOGIC

Use deductive logic to complete the grid so that each row, each column, and each 3×3 box contains the numbers 1 through 9 in some order. The solution is unique.

7	4			2	5			
					7	4	5	
							7	2
		2	6			8		
5		6		1		7		9
		7			8	6		
2	3							
	5	9	7					
		8	5				6	3

Four-Letter Anagrams

LANGUAGE

Fill in the blanks in each sentence below with words that are anagrams (rearrangements) of one another.

1. We could smell the foul __odor__ as soon as we opened the barn __door__ .

2. When the chef tried to carry a stack of _____, one _____ off and made a terrible clang.

3. The _____ of the litter waited for his _____ at the food dish.

4. The actor portrayed his _____ so well that he had the _____ attention of the audience.

5. When Sally's boyfriend gave her a _____, she had a happy _____ on her face.

6. The street _____ cast strange shadows through the leaves of the _____ tree.

7. The _____ letter was _____ an insurance company.

8. As the woman tried to keep _____ with her friend, the wind blew her _____ around her.

Answers on page 181.

Problematic Pool Hall

The kid was trying his best to beat the old-time master. But something was peculiar, something was wrong. We count 8 wrong things in this pool hall. How many can you find?

Four Square

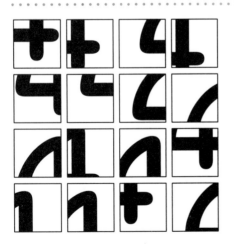

Each of the 16 square tiles shown in the illustration contains some part of the number 4. Select the 4 tiles that can create a 2×2 square so that a full "4" character appears on it. Tiles should not be rotated, flipped, or overlapped.

Answers on pages 181–182.

Mirror, Mirror

There's no trick here, only a challenge: Draw the mirror image of these familiar objects. You may find it harder than you think!

Decorative Word Search ATTENTION VISUAL SEARCH

Every word listed is contained within the box of letters below. The words can be found in a straight line horizontally, vertically, or diagonally. They may read either backward or forward.

BEDROOMS

CABINETS

CARPENTER

CARPETS

CEILING

CHANDELIER

CHEST

COLOR SWATCHES

CONSOLE

COST

CURTAINS

DESIGNER

ENTRY

FENG SHUI

FIXTURES

FLOOR PLANS

GARDEN

GLASS

HALLWAY

HOME OFFICE

HUTCH

LIGHT

PAINT

PATIO

RUGS

SCONCES

SET

SHADES

SHELF

SLIPCOVERS

SOFA

SPACE

TELEVISION

WALLPAPER

WALL UNITS

```
S E S C O N S O L E N T R Y Y
N C M H A O I T A P M W C A L
I A O A N B B V N R G A O W F
A P O N Z E I Y E I R L L L E
T S R D C X D N Q P A L O L N
R F D E K E G R E W F P R A G
U I E L M I S N A T O A S H S
C X B I S G T L N G S P W V H
A T L E U E L T S O C E A U U
R U D R R U L I G H T R T X I
P R J G N I L I E C A C C C S
E E C I F F O E M O H D H H S
T S T E L E V I S I O N E E A
S S Q S R E V O C P I L S S L
C S N A L P R O O L F D H T G
```

Answers on page 182.

What a Whistle, Part 1

Read the story that follows. Then turn the page for a quiz on what you've read.

When I was 14, I used to hang out at a nature center in Connecticut, where I grew up.

One day a man brought in a sparrow hawk with a busted wing. These days the official name of the bird is the American kestrel, but they will always be sparrow hawks to me. Anyway, it was a little beauty, a small falcon about the size of a jay, with beautiful colors—blue-gray wings, rufous tail and back—and that piercing gaze of hawks.

One of the curators, Les, took care of the sparrow hawk for a few months, feeding it small strips of raw meat. As the bird's wing grew stronger, Les started re-training it to fly indoors, holding a piece of meat in a gloved hand. He'd stand close at first, so the bird could practically jump to his hand, but then he'd stand farther and farther away. Soon the little hawk was flying to him for the food.

Each time Les held out the food, he'd do this remarkable whistle, which he said was the sound of a screech owl. It had a slightly eerie, tremulous sound. You do the whistle by fluttering the back of your tongue loosely against your palate. It's hard to explain. I practiced a lot, and soon I could do it too. People always seem surprised at the sound— it's not a typical whistle. You can vary the pitch to high or low by how you flutter your tongue. I don't have a lot of talents, but by gum I can do the screech-owl whistle!

What a Whistle, Part 2

(Do not read this until you have read the previous page!)

1. In which state did the author grow up?

2. Another name for the "sparrow hawk" is:
   a) blue grouse
   b) American kestrel
   c) purple finch

3. How old is the author at the time of the story?

4. True or false: The sparrow hawk has greenish wings.

5. Sparrow hawks in captivity can be fed:
   a) celery
   b) potatoes
   c) raw meat

6. The sparrow hawk in the story had:
   a) a bad wing
   b) a broken leg
   c) missing tail feathers

7. The sparrow hawk is a type of:
   a) shore bird
   b) falcon
   c) jay

8. As the bird healed, the curator:
   a) let it go
   b) retrained it to fly
   c) took it home

9. The curator trained the bird by using:
   a) a certain whistle
   b) a clucking sound
   c) a duck decoy

10. The sound the curator made was that of:
    a) a bald eagle
    b) a screech owl
    c) a barn owl

Answers on page 182.

Times Square

Fill in each empty cell of the grid with a number 1 through 9. The product (multiplication) of the numbers in each row must be the value to the right of that row of the grid, and the product of each column must be the value below that column of the grid. Important: the number 1 can only be used once in any row or column; other numbers can be repeated.

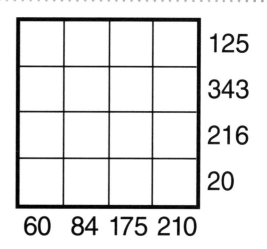

Star Power

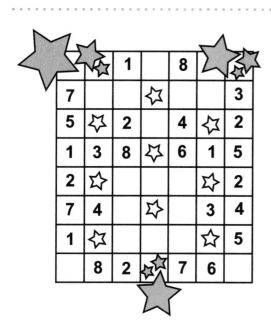

Fill in the empty cells of the grid so that each white star is surrounded by the digits 1 through 8 with no repeats.

Answers on page 182.

Sister's Brothers

Diane has no sisters, but her brother Wayne has one more brother than he has sisters. How many brothers does Diane have?

Winter Evening

Ahh...a calm, relaxing evening by the fire...or is it? We count 7 things wrong in this picture. How many can you find?

Answers on page 182.

Fold-O-Rama Maze

START

FINISH

Answer on page 182.

CONDITION YOUR COGNITION

Starboard Course Maze

SPATIAL REASONING   PLANNING

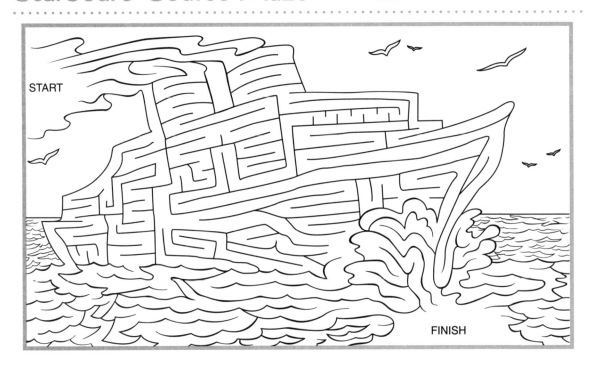

Alphabet Fill-In

LANGUAGE   LOGIC

The 8 five-letter words below are missing their first and last letters. Complete the words, using 16 different letters. We've filled in the S and D of SOLID to get you started, so now you may not use S or D in any of the other blanks.

1. __S O L I D__   2. __ A Y O __   3. __ E L A __   4. __ I L C __

5. __ H A K __   6. __ E N O __   7. __ U N T __   8. __ U E R __

Answers on page 183.

106

Name That Nickname

Five male friends are of different ages, go by different nicknames, drive different vehicles, have different jobs, and root for different pro football teams. Using the clues below, can you determine the age, vehicle, job, and favorite football team of the man nicknamed Tubba?

- The man who drives a station wagon roots for the Raiders.

- The man who drives a Hummer is 42.

- The man who roots for the Bengals is a flea trainer.

- The man who roots for the Cowboys has a 2-year age difference with the competitive eater.

- The man who drives an SUV is a toothpick tester.

- The man who drives an RV has a 2-year age difference with the 40-year-old.

- The man who roots for the Browns is nicknamed Dubba.

- The oldest man is 4 years older than the apple dewormer.

- The 38-year-old man roots for the Steelers.

- The man whose age is in the middle is an apple dewormer.

- The man nicknamed Rubba has a 2-year age difference with the man who roots for the Steelers.

- The man who drives an RV is the youngest.

- The 44-year-old man is a beer-bottle capper.

- The man who roots for the Cowboys has a 2-year age difference with the man nicknamed Hubba.

- The man who drives a pickup is nicknamed Bubba.

Answers on page 183.

Four Sisters

Upon her return from living abroad, Alberta, the youngest of 4 sisters, announced her shipboard marriage. Her 3 sisters, Carla, Paula, and Roberta were amazed by her husband's name. With the aid of the clues below determine Alberta's husband's first and last name, as well as Carla's, Paula's, and Roberta's husbands' first and last names. The 4 men are Albert, Carl, Paul, and Robert. Their last names are Albertson, Carlson, Paulson, and Robertson.

1. No woman's husband has a first name that consists of her first name without the final "a"; no woman's last name consists of her first name without the final "a" and with "son" on the end; and no man's last name consists of his first name with "son" added at the end.

2. Paul is not married to Roberta, and Robert is not married to Paula.

3. No husband and wife have "bert" in both of their first names, but there is a man who has "bert" in his first and last names.

4. Carl's last name is not Paulson.

	ALBERT	CARL	PAUL	ROBERT	ALBERTSON	CARLSON	PAULSON	ROBERTSON
ALBERTA								
CARLA								
PAULA								
ROBERTA								
ALBERTSON								
CARLSON								
PAULSON								
ROBERTSON								

Answers on page 183.

Number Crossword

Fill in this crossword with numbers instead of letters. Use the clues to determine which of the numbers 1 through 9 belongs in each square. No zeros are used.

Across

1. The square root of 2-Down
3. A multiple of 7
5. Its digits are in ascending order (not consecutive)
6. The square root of 3-Down

Down

1. Consecutive even digits, ascending
2. A square
3. A square
4. A square

Bookend Letters

Each word below is missing a pair of identical letters. Add the same letter to the beginning and end of each word to create new words. Do not use any pair of letters twice.

___ANGLE___

___CLIPS___

___RIM___

___TRAIT___

Answers on page 183.

Sevens

Across

1. Gowns
8. Sedative
15. Distributed the deck again
16. Akin
17. Ready, willing, ___
18. Standing up
19. More tired
20. Speeder's speed, perhaps
21. Queen ___ lace
23. Melody
24. Walks nervously
26. Guiding light
31. Mists
32. Antisocial one
33. One ___ time
34. Six make an inning
35. Lawn machine
36. Story basis
37. Exploit
38. Paddy crops
39. Monotonous hum
40. Goes over again
42. Actress Dunne
43. Cinder
44. Sagas
46. Brainier
50. Kitchen appliance
54. Italian dessert
55. Citrus drink
56. Changed
57. Warned
58. Yellowstone attractions
59. Deteriorates

Down

1. Sketch
2. Philosopher Descartes
3. Norse epic
4. Some regattas
5. Roman victims of 290 B.C.
6. Burstyn and DeGeneres
7. Cubic meter
8. Bikini halves
9. He enjoys novels twice
10. Famed portrayer of Hamlet
11. Electromagnetic wave amplifiers
12. "To put ___ a nutshell . . ."
13. Impression
14. Nervous
22. Most snaillike
24. Take a short break
25. Mexican native
27. Wallet fillers
28. Claw
29. Make amends
30. Velocity
31. Time unit
32. Door feature
35. Author of "The Covenant"
36. Mangle operators
38. Make like new
39. Visionary

41. Author Bret, et al
42. Philippine city with a repetitive name
45. Counselor-___
46. Buck
47. Burrower

48. Bohemian
49. Frees (of)
51. London gallery
52. Actress Barbara
53. Ohio team

Answers on page 183.

It's White

ATTENTION   **LANGUAGE**   **VISUAL SEARCH**

Every word listed is contained within the box of letters below. The words can be found in a straight line horizontally, vertically, or diagonally. They may read either backward or forward.

BAKING SODA

BONE

DANDRUFF

DIAPER

EGGS

FLOUR

GHOST

GOLF BALL

ICEBERG

IVORY

MERINGUE

MILK

PAPER

PING-PONG BALL

SALT

SANTA'S BEARD

SHEET

SNOW

SUGAR

TEETH

UNICORN

WHIPPED CREAM

WHITEWASH

```
W  P  P  S  W  A  K  I  N  I  V  O  R  Y  E
H  C  I  O  N  H  L  E  A  R  N  B  E  B  P
I  U  N  D  A  N  I  P  P  I  O  N  P  A  L
P  S  G  O  O  D  M  T  R  A  N  C  A  K  E
P  A  P  S  G  G  E  X  E  C  U  T  I  I  Y
E  N  O  B  L  E  R  S  T  W  S  P  D  N  R
D  T  N  U  T  P  I  U  T  R  A  I  L  G  U
C  A  G  H  F  Y  N  G  Y  P  O  S  T  S  O
R  S  B  O  L  F  G  A  E  T  I  E  H  O  L
E  B  A  J  L  N  U  R  A  C  T  E  C  D  F
A  E  L  S  T  F  E  R  E  O  E  S  P  A  T
M  A  L  A  D  O  B  B  D  T  T  R  O  O  F
D  R  Y  M  A  R  E  A  E  N  C  P  I  H  W
A  D  O  R  A  R  L  S  L  I  A  I  N  O  G
C  O  N  P  G  E  T  S  A  L  T  D  I  C  E
```

Answers on page 183.

Word Square and Memory Check, Part I

First, spend 2 minutes looking at the words in this crossword square. Then turn the page for a quiz.

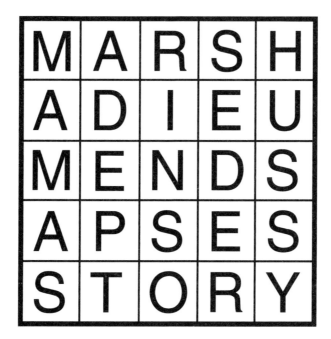

Trivia on the Brain

Scientists aren't sure how many brain cells you lose each day because of decay and misuse, but you don't need to worry: You have enough to last your whole lifetime!

Word Square and Memory Check, Part 2

MEMORY

(Don't look at this page until you've looked at page 113!)

Do you have those words memorized? Good. Now look at the list below and circle the words that appeared in the crossword square.

HARSH

MINDS

LENDS

ADIEU

FUSSY

STORY

GLORY

HUSSY

INEPT

RINSO

SEVER

PAPAS

MAMAS

HISSY

APSES

Answers on page 183.

Our Loopy Lingo

Rearrange the tiles to produce a head-scratching question.

Hint: It starts with the word "If."

N D S	H A	D E	O N E	H A	V E	D D S
I F	L B	Y O U	D G	T H	E T	F O
O F	U T	A T	E M ,	R I D	O F	W H
A N	Y O U	V E ?	D O	A B	A L	U N C
A N	H O					

Four Squares to Three

Reposition only 3 lines in order to make 3 squares of equal size.

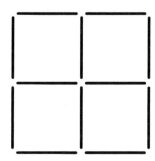

Answers on pages 183–184.

Deluge of Ds

How many things can you find in this picture that begin with the letter **D?** We count 14.

Bundle Up!

LANGUAGE   **PLANNING**

Change just one letter on each line to go from SCARF to GLOVE. Do not change the order of the letters. You must have a word at each step.

SCARF

_____

_____ to look intently

_____

_____

_____ musical hardwood stick

_____

GLOVE

Answers on page 184.

Pretzel Logic

Arrange each of the numbers 1 through 9 in the small circles below so that any 5 numbers around a larger circle add up to 22. Use each number only once. Can you come up with more than one solution?

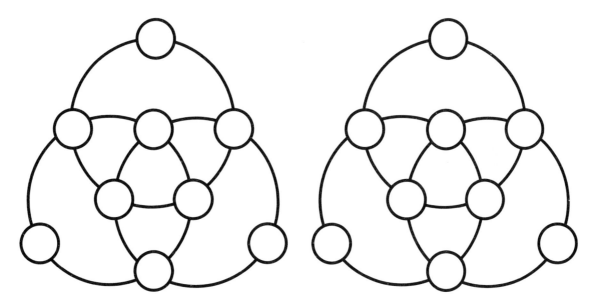

How Many Rectangles?

How many rectangles of all sizes are formed by the lines in the figure below? Do not include any squares in your count.

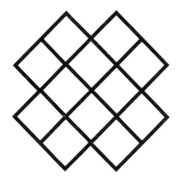

Answers on page 184.

Jelly Bean Jar Maze

To complete this sweet maze, find a path among the jelly beans to reach the other side of the candy jar.

Answer on page 184.

Sudoku

Use deductive logic to complete the grid so that each row, each column, and each 3×3 box contains the numbers 1 through 9 in some order. The solution is unique.

3	2				6			9
			5					3
						1		
8	3	2			9			
		7				9		
			1			6	3	8
		4						
9					7			
7			3				5	6

Fresh to Stale

Change just one letter on each line to go from the top word to the bottom word. Do not change the order of the letters. You must have a word at each step.

1. FRESH
_____
_____
_____
_____
_____
_____
_____
STALE

2. STICK
_____
_____
_____
STONE

3. LOSE
_____
_____
_____
FIND

Answers on page 184.

Perfect Square

Make 2 identical straight line cuts, one in each of the figures below, so that the resulting 4 pieces can be rearranged to form a perfect square.

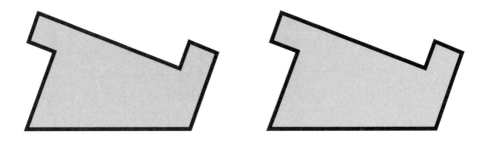

For Your Eyes Only

Look carefully at the 4 arrows below. Which one is the shortest? Which one is the longest? Are they all the same length? No need to use a ruler. Just use your eyes.

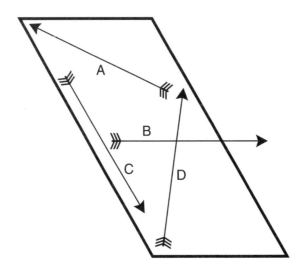

Answers on page 184.

Rhyme Time

Answer each clue below with a pair of rhyming words. The numbers that follow each clue indicate how many letters are in each word. For example, "Cookware taken straight from the oven" (3, 3) would be "hot pot."

1. Subdued startled reaction (4, 3)_____

2. Dull colored crustacean (4, 4)_____

3. Fail to keep up (4, 5)_____

4. Shine sufficiently (4, 6)_____

5. Sophisticated lad (5, 5)_____

6. Dog bark (5, 5)_____

7. Redundant sort of cliff (5, 6)_____

8. Pious pathfinder (6, 5)_____

9. Visitor roster (7, 4)_____

10. He takes you for an unhappy ride (6, 6)_____

11. Overfed pet (6, 5)_____

12. Heist featured on the big screen (7, 5)_____

13. Fountain drink fit for a king (7, 6)_____

14. Appliance deal (7, 7)_____

15. Entertainers at the ballpark (10, 4)_____

16. The road to the Final Four (7, 7)_____

Answers on page 184.

Executive Disorder

Even though there have been 43 presidents of the United States (at the time of this printing), there are only 37 different names on the list below. Do you know why? While you're thinking about it, put the 37 different names in the grid to the right.

4 Letters
BUSH
FORD
POLK
TAFT

5 Letters
ADAMS
GRANT
HAYES
NIXON
TYLER

6 Letters
ARTHUR
CARTER
HOOVER
MONROE
PIERCE
REAGAN
TAYLOR
TRUMAN
WILSON

7 Letters
CLINTON
HARDING
JACKSON
JOHNSON
KENNEDY
LINCOLN
MADISON

8 Letters
BUCHANAN
COOLIDGE
FILLMORE
GARFIELD
HARRISON
MCKINLEY
VAN BUREN

9 Letters
CLEVELAND
JEFFERSON
ROOSEVELT

10 Letters
EISENHOWER
WASHINGTON

Answer on page 185.

Sock Drawer

Tiny Tom can barely reach into the top drawer of his highboy where he keeps his socks. He knows he has 11 pairs of black socks and 6 pairs of brown socks scattered in the drawer with no pairs knotted together. How many socks would he have to pull out of the drawer in order to get a matching pair?

Horde of Hs

ATTENTION   VISUAL SEARCH

We count 14 things in this picture that begin with the letter **H.** How many can you find?

Answers on page 185.

Decorating Dilemma

A strange letter arrived recently at the office of Black and Brown Interiors. The letter set the entire staff on its ear until Black and Brown visited the Davis house personally. It read:

Dear Sirs:

Everyone in my family wants to redecorate our rec room differently. Lee insists on having an entire wall finished with black-and-white carpeting. Like a checkerboard! My son protests such a wall. He's already told his friends that the room will be Day-Glo orange. Just right for his black light!

Dale and my daughter disagree with Leslie's choice to wallpaper the west wall. I want the whole room rustically paneled, but nobody will listen to me!

There's no phone in the rec room. An occupant in the bedroom next door is sick and tired of having people running up and down the stairs delivering phone messages. Our upstairs occupant refuses to run messages to the converted garage every time her brother's girlfriends call. The woman of the house says, "No messages!"

Help!

Sincerely yours,

Pat Davis

From this letter determine each family member's name, how he or she wants the rec room decorated, and the bedroom location of each individual. Note: Two individuals share a room.

	DAD	DAUGHTER	SON	MOM	REDECORATION B&W CARPET	DAY-GLO PAINT	PANELING	WALLPAPER	BEDROOM LOCATION CONVERTED GARAGE	ROOM NEXT DOOR	UPSTAIRS ROOM	W/ ONE OF THE ABOVE
DALE												
LEE												
LESLIE												
PAT												
CONVERTED GARAGE												
ROOM NEXT DOOR												
UPSTAIRS ROOM												
W/ ONE OF THE ABOVE												
B&W CARPET												
DAY-GLO PAINT												
PANELING												
WALLPAPER												

Answers on page 185.

Word Jigsaw

Fit the pieces into the frame to form common, uncapitalized words reading across and down crossword-style. There's no need to rotate the pieces; they'll fit as shown, with each piece used exactly once.

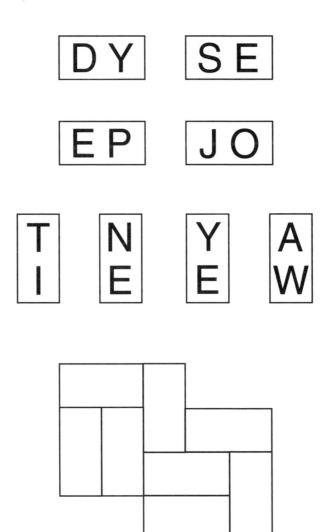

Answer on page 185.

ABCD

LOGIC   ATTENTION

Place the letter A, B, C, or D in each square of the grid. The tables above and to the left of the grid indicate how many times each letter appears in that column or row. No letter can be horizontally or vertically adjacent to itself.

				A	0	1	3	1	2	2
				B	2	2	0	2	1	2
				C	2	2	0	3	0	2
A	B	C	D	2	1	3	0	3	0
2	1	2	1							
1	3	1	1							
1	1	3	1							
2	2	0	2							
1	2	2	1							
2	0	1	3							

Geometric Shapes

LOGIC   SPATIAL REASONING

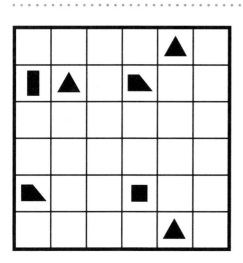

Divide the grid into smaller geometric shapes by drawing straight lines either following the grid lines or diagonally across the cells. Each formed shape must have exactly one symbol of the same shape inside it.

Answers on page 185.

Layer by Layer

Seventeen sheets of paper—each the same size and shape—were piled on a table. Number the sheets 1 through 17, with 1 as the top sheet and 17 as the bottom sheet.

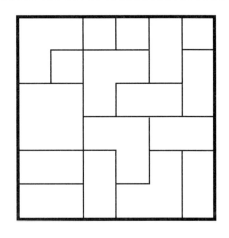

You Said It!

A cryptogram is a message in substitution code. Break the code to read the message. For example, THE SMART CAT might become FVO QWGDF JGF if F is substituted for T, V for H, O for E, and so on. The code is different for each cryptogram.

1. XG GXQ AQQIA OG YXGC TGD ARDQ CVJO

   SQGSKQ CJXO OVQAQ PJFA, QEMQSO OVJO OVQF

   CGX'O JMMQSO J SQXXF KQAA.

2. GYQKJ'F GCKTSDSCF XKTS NCYTSL GXKG GXS RYCDQ

   VF OSCGKVLDJ CYWLQ. VG VF GXSVC RKDDSGF

   GXKG KCS ZDKG.

Answers on page 186.

Mirror, Mirror

There's no trick here, only a challenge: Draw the mirror image of these familiar objects. You may find it harder than you think!

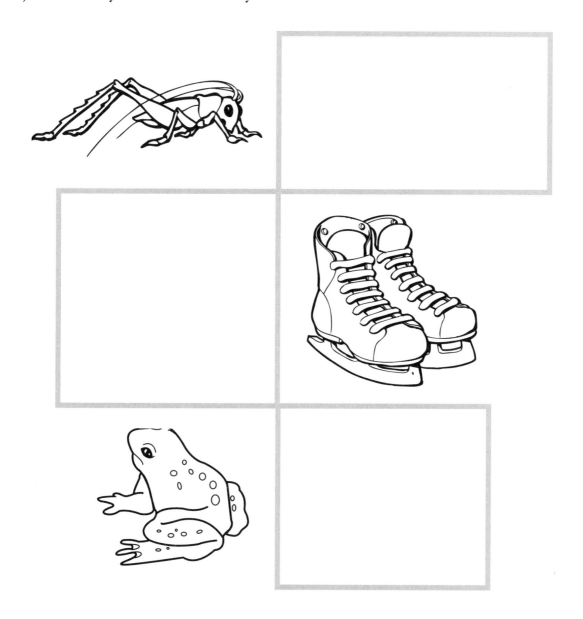

Shoot-out at the K.O. Corral

You've heard of the shoot-out at the O.K. Corral. But the shoot-out at the K.O. Corral? Now that was a strange scene. How many things in this picture don't make sense? We count 11.

Trivia on the Brain
The brain of a goldfish makes up 0.3% of its total body weight. An adult human brain is about 2% of total body weight.

Answers on page 186.

Sudoku

Use deductive logic to complete the grid so that each row, each column, and each 3×3 box contains the numbers 1 through 9 in some order. The solution is unique.

1	3					4		
			8					
	2	7			3		6	
			1		4	6		
	8			6			4	
		9	8		2			
	6		5			8	1	
				7				
		2				5	9	

Ideal Advice

Cryptograms are messages in substitution code. Break the code to read the message. For example, THE SMART CAT might become FVO QWGDF JGF if F is substituted for T, V for H, O for E, and so on. Hint: O equals N.

"HOI CA, JR NSDDAT HJSEBPHOC, HCY OAL

TMHL RAFE PAFOLER PHO IA NAE RAF; HCY

TMHL RAF PHO IA NAE RAFE PAFOLER."

—WAMO N. YSOOSIR

Answers on page 186.

Animal House

Across

1. Concordes: abbr.
5. Bass and treble
10. Teases
14. Lotion additive
15. Aged: Lat.
16. Concerning: Lat.
17. Biggest portion
19. Amateur sports grp.
20. Film editor's equipment
21. Owl hours
23. Paul, the guitar guy
24. Ready supply
26. Greek physician
29. Exclude
30. ___ plea (pleads guilty)
34. Mil. address
35. Greek flier
38. Pinches
39. Ivy League team
42. Ireland
43. Fuel vessel
44. Regret
45. Lots and lots: var.
47. Kleindienst, Kennedy, Civiletti, etc.
48. Beginning
50. O'Casey and Connery
52. One: Fr.
53. Dan, former CBS newsman
56. Mournful
60. Surrounding atmosphere
61. String game
64. Put away
65. Wipe out
66. Young adult
67. Make like a goose
68. Put off
69. Orient

Down

1. Mineo and Maglie
2. Sales receipt
3. Implement
4. Mentally deteriorated
5. Examples
6. Annealing oven
7. Timetable col.
8. Distant
9. Office skill, for short
10. Giant simian
11. Advance slowly
12. Mild oath
13. Oceans
18. Like some views
22. Trans. watchdogs
24. Polynesian garments
25. Ring apparel
26. Stares, openmouthed
27. March follower
28. French river
29. WWII battle site
31. Breakwaters
32. Mold opening

33. Plus quality
36. That: Fr.
37. Sault ___ Marie
40. Reporter
41. Presser
46. Match the bet
49. Nullify
51. Curved
52. Stomach ailment

53. Allergic reaction
54. Not manual
55. 1982 animated Disney feature
56. Being: Lat.
57. Concept
58. Pub drinks
59. Penny
62. 100 square meters
63. Make lace

Answers on page 186.

Entourage of Es

How many things within this picture begin with the letter **E**? We count 14. How many can you find?

Answers on page 186.

Weird Word Search, Part 1

Every word listed is contained within the box of letters below. The words can be found in a straight line horizontally, vertically, or diagonally. They may read either backward or forward. Be prepared to recognize these words again later.

ARCANE

BIZARRE

CHILLING

CREEPY

FREAKY

GHOSTLY

HAUNTED

MACABRE

SCARY

SPOOKY

STRANGE

SURREAL

UNCANNY

UNEARTHLY

```
P  A  F  R  E  A  K  Y  G  Y  S
W  U  Q  C  H  R  Y  M  O  L  P
B  Y  C  Y  H  A  B  F  D  H  O
I  L  Q  R  N  I  U  A  E  T  O
Z  T  Y  U  E  N  L  N  C  R  K
A  S  U  R  R  E  A  L  T  A  Y
R  O  D  A  A  C  P  C  I  E  M
R  H  U  F  R  C  I  Y  N  N  D
E  G  N  A  R  T  S  S  D  U  G
```

Answers on page 186.

Weird Word Search, Part 2

MEMORY

(Don't look at this page until you've completed the puzzle on page 135!)

Trick or treat! Circle the words from the list below that appeared in Weird Word Search, Part 1.

FANTASTIC	SUPERNATURAL
EERIE	PHANTASMAL
GHOSTLY	SPIRITUAL
UNCANNY	FREAKY
CHILLING	HALLOWEEN
SCARED	ARCANE
SÉANCE	HUNTED
BIZARRE	CREAKY
SHADOWY	MACABRE
STRANGE	SPECTER
CHILLY	WEIRD
UNREAL	CREEPY

Trivia on the Brain

The brain allows humans to distinguish between 3,000 and 10,000 different smells.

Answers on page 186.

Geometric Shapes

Divide the grid into smaller geometric shapes by drawing straight lines either following the grid lines or diagonally across the cells. Each formed shape must have exactly one symbol of the same shape inside it.

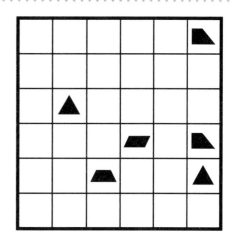

Letter Lesson

A cryptogram is a message in substitution code. Break the code to read the message. For example, THE SMART CAT might become FVO QWGDF JGF if F is substituted for T, V for H, O for E, and so on.

"ULT, VU DUAEVPB, OBD EDOODJ TBVWB FLPO

CJDIMDUOEQ LWWMJP VP D. YCODJTYJX, OBD

PMWWDPPVLU JMUP OBMP: Y, L, V, X, B, U, J, P, O, M,

Q, W, C, A, E, F, T, Z, G, K, I, S, R. D KJDXLFVUYODP

PL JDFYJGYZEQ, OBYO YU VUXVNVXMYE PDUODUWD LC

YUQ EDUAOB VP JYJDEQ PDDU, VU TBVWB VO VP ULO

OBD KJDNYVEVUA WBYJYWODJ."

—DXAYJ YEEYU KLD

Answers on pages 186–187.

Odd-Even Logidoku

The numbers 1 through 9 appear once in every row, column, long diagonal, and irregular shape. All cells marked with the letter E contain even numbers. From the numbers given, can you complete the puzzle?

Layer by Layer

SPATIAL REASONING   CREATIVE THINKING

Twelve sheets of paper—each the same size and shape—were piled on a table. Number the sheets 1 through 12, with 1 as the top sheet and 12 as the bottom sheet.

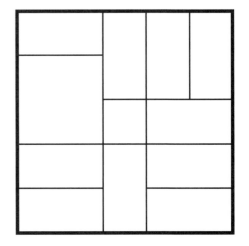

Answers on page 187.

138

EXERT YOUR INTELLECT

Charmer Maze

PLANNING   SPATIAL REASONING

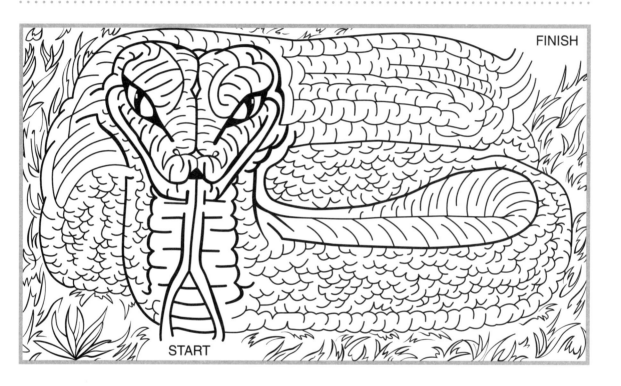

FINISH

START

Bookend Letters

LANGUAGE

Each word below is missing a pair of identical letters. Add the same letter to the beginning and end of each word to create new words. Do not use any pair of letters twice.

1. ___EARL___

2. ___ELUDE___

3. ___EVOLVE___

4. ___EAT___

5. ___EVE___

6. ___EURO___

Answers on page 187.

139

The Morning Landscape

Sean, a local landscaper, made a startling discovery as he prepared for his Monday morning deliveries. He had received orders for 4 trees: an apple, an elm, a maple, and a pear. The 4 customers were the Browns, the Greens, the Greys, and the Whites. As Sean mapped out his delivery route, he noticed that the addresses of the 4 customers had the same names as the trees he had to deliver: Apple Lane, Elm Drive, Maple Lane, and Pear Drive. Using the information below, determine the order in which the deliveries were made, in whose yard each tree was planted, and on what street.

1. The Grey family does not live on Apple Lane.

2. No tree was planted on a street bearing its name, but one fruit tree was planted on a street bearing the name of the other fruit tree.

3. Sean planted the maple tree later than he planted a tree at the Browns' house but earlier than he planted a tree at either address followed by the word "Drive."

4. He did not plant the pear tree on a street followed by the word "Lane," but he planted it before his stop at the White's house.

	APPLE TREE	ELM TREE	MAPLE TREE	PEAR TREE	APPLE LANE	ELM DRIVE	MAPLE LANE	PEAR DRIVE	BROWN	GREEN	GREY	WHITE
FIRST												
SECOND												
THIRD												
FOURTH												
BROWN												
GREEN												
GREY												
WHITE												
APPLE LANE												
ELM DRIVE												
MAPLE LANE												
PEAR DRIVE												

Answers on page 187.

LANGUAGE

Shakespeare's Women

ATTENTION   VISUAL SEARCH

Every word listed is contained within the box of letters below. The words can be found in a straight line horizontally, vertically, or diagonally. They may read either backward or forward. The leftover letters spell the name of another one of Shakespeare's female characters (18 letters).

ALICE

ANDROMACHE

ANNE PAGE

AUDREY

BEATRICE

CASSANDRA

CELIA

CERES

CLEOPATRA

CORDELIA

CRESSIDA

DESDEMONA

DIANA

DOLL TEARSHEET

ELEANOR

ELIZABETH

EMILIA

GONERIL

```
L A R T A P O E L C L S R M L
J U L I E T G A C E D O I A E
U T C E T A C E H E N Y D R L
N N E E P E R C Y A R Y R I I
O P H E L I A O E N M E O N Z
R S N N H M T L L A C H S A A
C N A E O S E E C I R T A E B
A U D R E Y R B L R R N L U E
S D D I I A E A A A O E I I T
S N I S A T I I E M M E N M H
A N S S H N L L E T B M E O E
N A A A S U A D E R L I L G G
D O B G J E S S I C A L A E N
R J E D E E R H E R M I O N E
A I L E D R O C M I R A N D A
```

HECATE	JESSICA	LUCE	PERCY (Lady)
HERMIONE	JOAN	MARIANA	REGAN
IMOGEN	JULIA	MARINA	ROSALINE
IRAS	JULIET	MIRANDA	_____
IRIS	JUNO	NERISSA	
ISABEL	LADY MACBETH	OPHELIA	

Answers on page 187.

Wise Words

A cryptogram is a message in substitution code. Break the code to read the message. For example, THE SMART CAT might become FVO QWGDF JGF if F is substituted for T, V for H, O for E, and so on. The code is different for each cryptogram.

1. JIRY IB VR GCQ EIFGE—ZSQH ZQ CQGMS G

   MQCYGAH GUQ, ZQ EAWQ YI RYAMW

   YI AY.

2. YZV YZPGWB KCBY UVCUSV JQGY YC AGCJ QTV

   GCGV CM YZVPT IFBPGVBB.

3. EYQRUEX UC UAMYCCUJSL QY QRL ABE ZRY

   PYLCE'Q RBGL QY PY UQ RUACLSV.

4. EFVAUVAY GBOO VX GVXB; SOCAAVAY GBOO VX

   GVXBN; MHVAY GBOO VX GVXBXE CAM PBXE HR

   COO.

5. JIX LZY BFFT JIXK WFZC ZMIAF NZRFK OS JIX

   WIDC JIXK LWOY XT.

Answers on pages 187–188.

Kingdom of Ks

We count 10 things in this picture that begin with the letter **K.** How many can you find?

Answers on page 188.

Mister Ed-ucation

Across

1. Admit
6. Reverse or neutral
10. Norwegian metropolis
14. From Rome (prefix)
15. Crucifix inscription
16. Atop of
17. Take it off
18. Rivers of comedy
19. Price displayers
20. Cuties that lack depth?
22. Garfield's sidekick
23. Raw metal
24. Trick shot in a film, e.g.
26. Visit briefly
30. Emphatic turndown
32. Duct drop
33. Sky sightings
35. Horizontal line on a graph
39. K-12, textbook-wise
40. Kind of tournament
42. Storied captain
43. Cap attachment
45. New Age music superstar
46. Nibble, beaver style
47. Weather, in a way
49. Wishful thinking
51. Boardroom echoes
54. "Diamonds ___ Forever"
55. Keen on
56. Mister Ed-ucation?

63. Alt.
64. Part of a Faulkner title
65. Online letters
66. Superman's lady
67. Model airplane builder's need
68. Capone colleague
69. Fashion's Christian
70. Sentry's cry
71. Elders and alders

Down

1. Talk like Daffy Duck
2. Place in a Robert Redford movie
3. Canvas covering
4. Former netman Nastase
5. "Piece of cake"
6. Toy soldier
7. Chemical compound
8. Uzbekistan border sea
9. Salon jobs
10. Where to take the roast?
11. Bogart sleuth
12. Mr. Spock's strong suit
13. Advent
21. Wither
25. Tricky situation
26. Remarriage prefix
27. Fabled archer
28. Surfer's paradise
29. Top van driver?
30. Everybody's opposite
31. Anthem opening

34. Ricky's landlord
36. "___: Warrior Princess"
37. Mosque V.I.P.
38. Pen mothers
41. Bebé holder
44. Poet's before
48. In the heavens
50. Mind terribly
51. Give up
52. Communist leader Zhou ___

53. Kind of pad or pool
54. Up to the present
57. Earthenware jar
58. Julia of Hollywood
59. Bahrain biggie
60. Corddry of "Studio 60 on the Sunset Strip"
61. Building location
62. Tigers foe

Answers on page 188.

Straight Line Challenge

Divide the square below into 16 pieces using 5 straight lines. Each piece should contain only one letter.

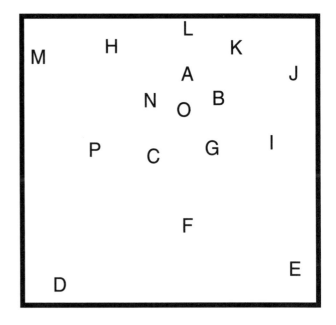

Plant Life

Some words related to plants are "planted" in this grid. To spell a word, start at any letter and move from letter to letter by traveling to any adjacent letter—up, down, across, or diagonally—but do not come back to a letter you've used previously in that word. Can you find 10 plant words of at least four letters each?

P M K R A
E L F O B
T A I L W
S U G E R
B H R N F

Answers on page 188.

It's a Shore Thing, Part 1

This private beach has an unusual "entrance fee": Before you can use the beach, you have to take a memory test given by the beach patrol. Study this picture for 2 minutes, then turn the page and answer the 10 questions. Seven or more right answers gets a free beach permit for the day!

It's a Shore Thing, Part 2

(Do not read this until you have read the previous page!)

The beach patrol asks you the following questions:

1. What toy were the kids in the water throwing? _____

2. What was the girl with the braids holding? _____

3. What was the name of the lotion the woman was applying? _____

4. What was the design on the same woman's swimsuit? _____

5. The float in the water was shaped like what kind of animal? _____

6. What was the name of the sailboat? _____

7. What had the angler caught? _____

8. What 3 types of clothing were worn by the man holding hands? _____

9. What did the lifeguard have slung over his shoulder? _____

10. How many birds were in the picture? _____

A Bright Idea

LOGIC   **CREATIVE THINKING**

A billionaire offered 3 men this challenge: "The man who can fill this room with something using the least amount of money will win a million dollars." The first man spent $25 and filled the room with lots of air-filled balloons. The second man spent $250 and filled the room with a single, giant air-filled balloon. The third man spent nothing and won the million dollars. What did he do?

Answers on page 188.

Numerical Word Search

This word search differs from the norm. Do not search for the actual digits in the word list. Instead, look for the spelling of each digit as it relates to each word. The first word, for example, is BALFOUR. All of the words have numbers within them, though they may not sound like that number when pronounced.

BAL 4 (Earl of)

CYCL 1

DRIF 2 OD

11SES

5 FOLD

FORGOT 10

FR 8 ER

H 8 S

L 1 SOME

M 1 TARY

M 1 Y

9 PINS

N 1

1 ROUS

ROT 10

```
N O I S N E T T O G R O F I V
S E I T N E V E S N T D L O T
S I S O T H P R G H E I G E N
A T D I O L I V G L I R N F E
T N H L X D E I C O R D O O X
U F E G D S E E Y D E O R U Y
R R O G I L H E C R F O U R S
N E M O S E N O L R O W O R I
I I O K B O H O O E W T F A X
N G N E M N I T N T T F L G P
E H E E V N G B E E E I A E E
L T T L P O R T N C B R B R N
I E A O F I V E F O L D C E C
G R R E N I N H C Y R T S O E
D E Y I N S E S N E V E L E L
```

SATUR 9

7 TIES

6 PENCE

6-SHOOTER

SL 8

STRYCH 9

10 DERLOIN

10 SION

2 FER

UND 1

Answers on page 188.

Six-String Maze

PLANNING   SPATIAL REASONING

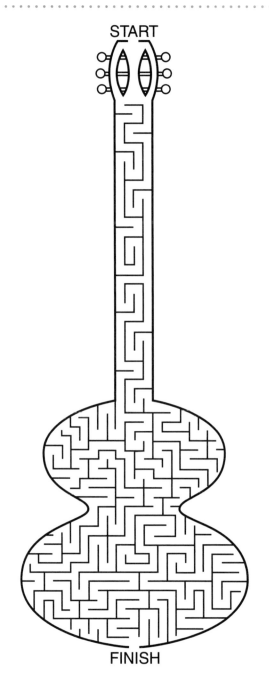

Answer on page 188.

Swarm of Ss

ATTENTION   **VISUAL SEARCH**

We count 19 things in this picture that begin with the letter **S.** How many can you find?

LANGUAGE

Word of Mouth

ATTENTION   **VISUAL SEARCH**

Some words related to the mouth are hidden in this grid. To spell a word, start at any letter and move from letter to letter by traveling to any adjacent letter—up, down, across, or diagonally—but do not come back to a letter you've used previously in that word. Can you find 11 mouth-y words?.

T E A L L
H P E A I
A U T S M
R G O P A
S I N Y T

Answers on page 188.

Movie Weekend

Skip and Sissy are avid movie fans. But they live so far from a town with movie theaters that when they're in town for a weekend, they try to see as many films as possible. Last weekend they saw movies on Saturday night and Sunday night, as well as matinees on both days. They went to all 4 theaters in town: the Bijou, the Jewel, the Odeon, and the Plaza. The 4 movies were directed by Woody Allen, Robert Altman, Mel Brooks, and François Truffaut. The movies were as different as their directors: a comedy, a mystery, a science fiction, and a western. Using the information given below, determine when and where Skip and Sissy saw each film and who directed it.

1. Skip and Sissy saw the science-fiction movie later than the comedy but earlier than the movie playing at the Jewel. None of these films was directed by Robert Altman.

2. They didn't go to a matinee at the Plaza.

3. They saw the Woody Allen film later than the comedy and earlier than the Truffaut movie, but none of these 3 films played at the Bijou.

4. They saw the Mel Brooks movie later than the western.

	BIJOU	JEWEL	ODEON	PLAZA	COMEDY	MYSTERY	SCIENCE FICTION	WESTERN	ALLEN	ALTMAN	BROOKS	TRUFFAUT
SAT. MATINEE												
SAT. NIGHT												
SUN. MATINEE												
SUN. NIGHT												
ALLEN												
ALTMAN												
BROOKS												
TRUFFAUT												
COMEDY												
MYSTERY												
SCIENCE FICTION												
WESTERN												

Answers on page 189.

Sudoku

Use deductive logic to complete the grid so that each row, each column, and each 3×3 box contains the numbers 1 through 9 in some order. The solution is unique.

	4		5		3			
		8		7				4
3		5		2				7
		2						
		6	1		8	2		
						5		
4				8		9		1
8				5		6		
			9		2		8	

Hex Dissection

Cut the figure into 3 parts following the grid lines. The parts are equal in size and shape, but they may be rotated or mirrored.

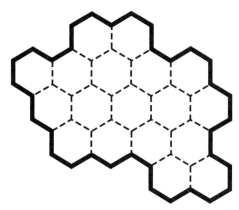

Answers on page 189.

Exert Your Intellect

Sawtooth Cube

Which two cubes can be unwrapped to form the pattern in the center?

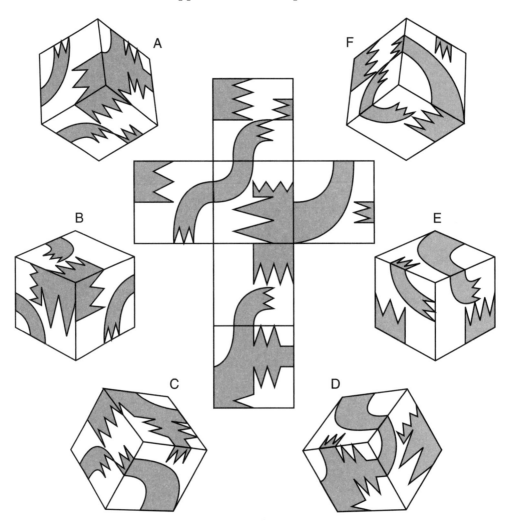

Answers on page 189.

154

Password Maker, Part 1

Most of us have a computer these days, and most programs require a password. What's your method of coming up with one? To make the password easy to remember, most people use some combination of their initials and birthday. But that also makes it easier for someone else to guess. One good method is to put together two unrelated words, like **JOKER CAMEL** or **TRUMPET ANKLE.** No need to work hard at that, though, because we're going to give you 10 good passwords at no charge! Read this list over a few times, then turn the page.

ADVICE KETTLE

PIANO LOBSTER

BELIEF HAMMER

FREEDOM ELEPHANT

CONCEPT SALAMANDER

PRESTIGE NINETEEN

FLUTTER CAMPUS

QUOTATION ORANGE

COWBOY GOLDEN

MOUNTAIN CYMBAL

Password Maker, Part 2

MEMORY

(Don't look at this until you've looked at the words on page 155!)

Now that you've looked at the list for a few minutes, here are the passwords again, in random order. Can you remember at least 8 word pairs?

_____ GOLDEN   ADVICE _____

FREEDOM _____   _____ LOBSTER

_____ ORANGE   PRESTIGE _____

FLUTTER _____   _____ HAMMER

_____ CYMBAL   CONCEPT _____

Alternate Corners

SPATIAL REASONING

Draw a single closed loop passing through each cell of the grid exactly once and moving only horizontally and vertically. Every second corner of the loop is on a circle, and each circle is a corner. Every other corner is on an empty cell.

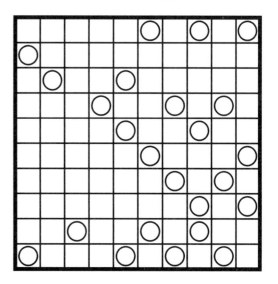

Answers on page 189.

Mirror, Mirror

There's no trick here, only a challenge: Draw the mirror image of these familiar objects. You may find it harder than you think!

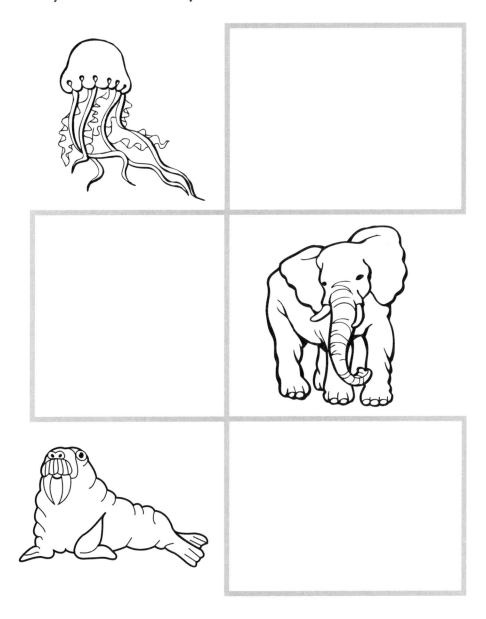

Lost Weekend

Across

1. Celeb.
4. Invitation letters
8. Fresh and firm
13. Dutch cheese
15. Lamb pen name
16. Tissue: pref.
17. Roller coaster, e.g.
18. ___ irae: Lat.
19. Avoid
20. New Orleans thoroughfare
23. Fending (off)
24. Landed property
27. Fidgety
30. Wernher ___ Braun
31. Plus
35. Grief
36. ___ of clay
37. Salinger novel, with "The"
41. Rugged rock
42. Diamond ___
43. Possessor
44. Stool pigeon
45. Tendency to face facts
48. Lacking in vitality
50. The whole ___
55. Highland dog
58. Overflowed
60. Sound of laughter
61. Concept
62. Character in "Rain"
63. Moslem prince
64. Williams and Knight
65. Belonging to them
66. Crockett portrayer Parker
67. Draft initials

Down

1. Action words
2. Dunce
3. Italian commune
4. Made over
5. Throws
6. Competes
7. Gone by
8. Photographer's word
9. Fastener
10. "There ___ in the town"
11. Rule: abbr.
12. Edgar Allan
14. Griffin of game shows
21. Inception
22. Face with masonry
25. Seeing eye ___
26. Stage direction
28. Woven fabric
29. Atom with net electric charge
31. Ghana capital
32. See-through brand
33. Home, to U.S. soldiers abroad
34. Hosp. test
36. Not many

38. Choose
39. Inlet
40. Four bagger
45. Reveler gone amok
46. "What ___ Thing Called Love?"
47. Clips
49. 1152, to Cato
51. English person

52. Helpers
53. Requires
54. Ground cover
56. Cook
57. Harness part
58. Concorde, e.g.
59. Exclamation of disgust

Answers on page 189.

Headline Howlers

Cryptograms are messages in substitution code. Break the code to read the message. For example, THE SMART CAT might become FVO QWGDF JGF if F is substituted for T, V for H, O for E, and so on. The code is the same for each cryptogram below.

1. CGYW QVCB FZJIGJGEZW WFVMCW.

2. IBY JVDB OEXYW ZD FBK SIGYHBW.

3. VWJIEFVZJ JVCBW SXVQB PEI HVW GF

   WDVMBMIVPJ.

4. DXVFB JEE MXEWB JE HIEZFY, MIVWO DIESB JEXY.

Geometric Shapes

Divide the grid into smaller geometric shapes by drawing straight lines either following the grid lines or diagonally across the cells. Each formed shape must have exactly one symbol of the same shape inside it.

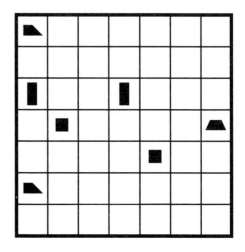

Answers on page 189.

Fabulous Creatures

No Loch Ness monster or Bigfoot here, but these mostly amiable beasts are indeed fabulous—that is, they're creatures of fable. Do you remember what they're called? Decipher the anagrams and match them to the pictures.

1. COIN URN

2. DOG RAN

3. AIM TO RUN

4. RAN CUTE

5. I'M DREAM

6. GIN RIFF

A.

B.

C.

D.

E.

F.

Answers on page 189.

Logidoku

The numbers 1–8 appear once in every row, column, long diagonal, irregular shape, and 2×4 rectangle. From the numbers given, can you complete the puzzle?

Layer by Layer

Seventeen sheets of paper—each the same size and shape—were piled on a table. Number the sheets 1 through 17, with 1 as the top sheet and 17 as the bottom sheet.

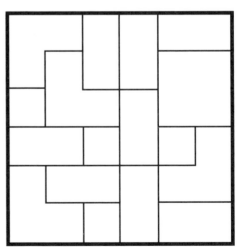

Answers on pages 189–190.

Forget-Me-Not and Friends, Part I

LOGIC   PLANNING   SPATIAL REASONING

We hereby nominate forget-me-not as the official flower of memory puzzles. Fill in the grid with the flower words. Look at the completed grid for 2 minutes and remember the 12 words, then turn the page for a quiz.

4 Letters

ALOE

5 Letters

DAISY

6 Letters

CACTUS

7 Letters

BOUQUET

JASMINE

8 Letters

DAFFODIL

HYACINTH

MAGNOLIA

MARIGOLD

9 Letters

BUTTERCUP

CARNATION

11 Letters

FORGET-ME-NOT

Answer on page 190.

Forget-Me-Not and Friends, Part 2

Circle the flower words that appeared in the grid on the previous page.

NOSEGAY

MAGNOLIA

LILAC

BUTTERCUP

JASMINE

LAVENDER

GLADIOLUS

DAFFODIL

CORNFLOWER

DAISY

FORGET-ME-NOT

JONQUIL

PERIWINKLE

CARNATION

PANSY

ALOE

Trivia on the Brain
The part of the brain called the amygdala gets its name from the Greek word for "almond" because of the similarities in shape.

Answers on page 190.

Made of Money

Every word listed is contained within the box of letters below. The words can be found in a straight line horizontally, vertically, or diagonally. They may read either backward or forward. The leftover letters spell a well-known expression (10 words).

BRASS

BREAD

CARTWHEEL

CENT

C-NOTE

COIN

CROWN

DIME

DINAR

DOLLAR

DOUBLE EAGLE

DOUBLOON

FARTHING

FIVE–SPOT

FLORIN

FRANC

GRAND

GREENBACKS

KRONE

LIRE

MARK

NGWEE

PENNY

PESO

POUND

QUARTER

QUID

RAND

RIYAL

RUBLE

RUPEE

SAWBUCK

TWO BITS

```
        R A N D I M E
       U G N I H T R A F
      B R T R H E Q L O R V
     L A E A D N U O P E P K O
    E N F L M C A R T W H E E L C
    D I L G B R E A D C O R N S R
    E O Y A T O P S E V I F K T O
    D C P E N N Y N I L S C T I W
    I O R E I G T R I Y A L H B N
    U E U L R W K C U B W A S O R
    Q E O B O E O T N O F F S W E
     A N U L E E E P U R S L T
      L O F O E D I N A R O
       D R R O E V R N N
        G K I N B L C
```

Answers on page 190.

As You Will

Across

1. Summer getaway
5. Prank
8. Sail supports
13. Khayyám
14. Elephant boy of the movies
15. Former USSR cooperative
16. Phrase that precedes for the better or for the worse
18. Meadow overpass
19. Rivals at war
20. Marked
22. Levin and Gershwin
23. "I get ___ out of you …"
24. Are suitable for
27. Estop, in law
30. Boston hrs.
31. Actress Eleonora, et al
33. Photo tone
34. Diamond or Young
36. Jumping sticks
38. Atmospheric pollution
39. Dais principal
41. Mountains of Utah
43. Summer quaff
44. Wrestling maneuver
46. Thinker, in a way
48. "The bald ___" (Dogpatch denizen)
49. Opposed, in 48-Across locale
50. Tests for better results
52. Milksops
56. Foreclose on ___
57. Be encouraged
59. Cohered
60. Flock members
61. Line a roof
62. Etta's cartoon relatives
63. Type of alert
64. Snack for José

Down

1. Where coos are heard
2. "___ for All Seasons"
3. Manufacture
4. Early newborn, for short
5. Electromagnetic unit
6. Cut sht.
7. Icelandic poet who wrote in Danish
8. Gummy substances
9. Items
10. Mugger, of a kind
11. Scope or photo start
12. Kane's Rosebud
14. Become misty
17. Ventilated
21. Greek or Turkish weight
24. "John Brown's Body" poet
25. Swelling
26. Stand pat
27. ___ the ring (schoolyard game)
28. Electron tube
29. Excited
32. Tar's hat
35. Opposing generals or actress's name

37. Smokes
40. Ruchings, e.g.
42. Foolishly imitative
45. Grand _____ Opry
47. Katydid, for one
49. Questioned

50. Pool hall equipment
51. She: Fr.
53. Nuclear watchdog grp.
54. Novelist Ambler
55. Town on the Vire
58. Overwhelm

Answers on page 190.

Sudoku

Use deductive logic to complete the grid so that each row, each column, and each 3×3 box contains the numbers 1 through 9 in some order. The solution is unique.

	6	5		4			7	1
8						1		
		3		9				
4		1	2					
	2			7			5	
					5	2		3
				8		9		
			6					7
	1	7		5		3	2	

A Gourmet Guide to Toad Egos

Make a meal of these TOAD EGOS (good eats) by finding the proper anagrams (rearrangements) of the capitalized words in the story below.

Rattling his pots and pans, Thomas Trencherman, master chef, addressed his class. "Snap to, my foodies, time for breakfast! For a snack with coffee, let's have some delicious PARTISAN DISHES _____. Now we'll go through an entire dinner menu, from ZIPPER TEA _____ to RED SETS _____. Let's start with a bowl of OUR UPS JUDO _____, which today is COLD-WAR CHEM, _____, then offer a chilled MICROCHIP STALK _____. Entrée choices will include FUN-FUR DARTS _____, consisting of medium-rare WINTRY POKERS _____, served with a steaming hot STARLET BOIL _____. For dessert, a choice of MAUI STIR _____ or the ever-popular EEL CEREBRUM _____. TIBETAN POP _____ to you!"

Answers on page 190.

REASSESS YOUR BRAIN

You have just completed a set of puzzles designed to challenge your various mental skills. We hope you enjoyed them. Did this mental exercise also improve your memory, attention, problem solving, and other important cognitive skills? To get a sense of your improvement, please fill out this questionnaire. It is exactly the same as the one you filled out before you worked the puzzles in this book. So now you can compare your cognitive skills before and after you embarked on a *Brain Games*™ workout.

The questions below are designed to test your skills in the areas of memory, problem solving, creative thinking, attention, language, and more. Please reflect on each question, and rate your responses on a 5-point scale, where 5 equals "excellent" and 1 equals "very poor." Then tally up your scores and check out the categories at the bottom of the next page to learn how you have sharpened your brain.

1. After attending a party where you meet 5 to 10 new and interesting people, how skilled are you at remembering their names the next day?

    1   2   3   4   5

2. When going to a new place for the first time, how confident are you that you'll remember the directions? If you often get lost, deduct a point from your score.

    1   2   3   4   5

3. How capable are you at planning your daily activities? Do you make a schedule and stick to it, or do you find yourself scrambling to get things done each day?

    1   2   3   4   5

4. Consider this scenario: You have a full day of meetings and events at work. Then an important client calls at the last minute to reschedule an appointment. How good are you at juggling your schedule to accommodate this unanticipated change?

    1   2   3   4   5

5. How well do you remember news stories? Can you remember in good detail at least three stories you read in the paper, heard on the news, or saw on television in the past 24 hours?

    1   2   3   4   5

6. Consider this scenario: You're working on an assignment with a tight deadline, but your brother keeps calling to ask you questions about the vacation you're taking together next month. Rate your ability to stay on task without getting distracted.

    1   2   3   4   5

7. When you're doing several different things at once—multitasking—do you feel that you are giving the appropriate amount of attention to each task? Say you're baking a cake, sorting the laundry, and having a phone conversation with your best friend. Can you have a good chat without burning the cake or accidentally putting a red sock in with your whites?

1   2   3   4   5

8. When you're trying to describe something, are you good at expressing yourself clearly and succinctly? Deduct points if you sometimes have trouble finding exactly the right word.

1   2   3   4   5

9. How good is your ability to do simple math in your head without using a calculator?

1   2   3   4   5

10. Consider this scenario: You're planning an anniversary party for your sister and are responsible for all the details, including food, entertainment, invitations, and venue. How good are you at this type of event planning? (If you could track down everything and throw a perfect party, give yourself a 5. If you're less organized and would end up forgetting to hire a caterer, give yourself a 1.)

1   2   3   4   5

10–25 Points:
Are You Ready to Make a Change?
Keep at it: There are plenty of activities that will help you improve your brain health! Continue working puzzles on a regular basis. Pick up another *Brain Games*™ book, and choose a different type of puzzle each day, or do a variety of them to help strengthen memory, focus attention, and improve logic and problem solving.

26–40 Points:
Building Your Mental Muscle
You're no mental slouch, but there's always room to sharpen your mind! Try to identify the types of puzzles that you found particularly difficult in this book. Then you'll get an idea of which cognitive skills you need to work on. Remember, doing a puzzle can be the mental equivalent of doing lunges or squats: While they might not be your first choice of activity, you'll definitely like the results!

41–50 Points:
View from the Top
Congratulations! You have finished the puzzles in this book and are performing like a champion. To maintain this level of mental fitness, keep challenging yourself by working puzzles every day. Like the rest of the body's muscles, your mental strength can decline if you don't use it. So choose to keep your brain strong and active. You're at the summit—now you just have to stay to enjoy the view!

ANSWERS

A-MAZE-ing Race (page 11)

Crossed Words (page 12)

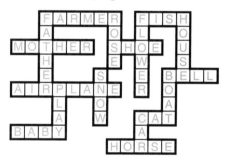

Soft to Hard (page 12)

SOFT, sort, sore, core, cord, card, HARD

Starburst (page 13)

Sudoku (page 13)

3	4	9	7	8	5	1	2	6
6	1	8	3	2	9	7	4	5
5	7	2	1	6	4	9	8	3
8	3	5	4	7	2	6	9	1
9	2	1	6	5	3	8	7	4
7	6	4	8	9	1	3	5	2
1	9	7	5	4	6	2	3	8
2	5	6	9	3	8	4	1	7
4	8	3	2	1	7	5	6	9

What's the Problem? (page 14)

$A + B + C = 10$; $A = 2$; $B = 3$; $C = 5$

Maze-l Tov! (page 14)

Types of Cake (page 15)

C O C O N U T O R R A C B P W
H H T J Y E L L O W E W A E B
I D O I Z E G D U F X Y N A I
F W R C U B T N N I S I A R R
F P H M O R D N O M L A N L T
O R U I O L F M A P L E A D H
N A P H T D A T E P S C N E A
L L S T Y E P T E E Y U O V Y
R I I R R O E Q E C B A M I I
E N D C U Z Z H F A Q S E L E
G E E N Z M C M F N M E L S N
N C D E G N A R O M U L P F O
I I O Y R R E H C C D P S O H
G P W E D D I N G Z H P D O H
Z S N D O O F L E G N A C D Y

171

Answers

Autumn Delight (pages 16–17)

T	A	R	P		C	A	P	E		C	A	B
O	L	E	O		O	L	A	V		A	L	A
F	A	L	L	I	N	G	L	E	A	V	E	S
U	S	A		T	E	A		N	I	E	C	E
		T	O	S	S		S	I	R			
O	B	I	T		E	O	N		S	P	A	
F	O	O	T	B	A	L	L	G	A	M	E	S
F	A	N		I	L	K		D	I	P	S	
		A	C	E		R	O	O	D			
S	H	A	D	Y		Y	O	W		G	O	T
N	E	W	S	C	H	O	O	L	Y	E	A	R
I	R	A		L	O	G	S		I	N	F	O
P	R	Y		E	D	I	T		P	S	S	T

Loop de Loop (page 18)

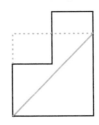

Where ARE They? (page 18)

17: On a dARE, CAREy called Marie, A REgular at his favorite bAR, Expecting to get her cell phone. Marie scAREs easily so she compAREd his number to her speed-dial list and didn't answer. CAREy ate a pear and decided to visit BAR, Ex-wife number two, but cAR Engine trouble forced him to take a cab and shARE fARE with a fair-haired lass named Clair, who told him he didn't have a prayer with her. Bar doesn't cARE for CAREy so she had current boyfriend Gary blARE A REd horn to scARE CAREy away.

Who's There? (page 19)

"Well, if I called the wrong number, why did you answer the phone?"
—James Thurber

Really Sum-thing (page 19)

One Cut (page 20)

An Arm and a Leg (page 20)

Your answers may vary.
1. ARM, aim, aid, lid, led, LEG
2. SOLE, sore, core, care, CARP
3. PLAY, slay, slap, slop, STOP
4. VEAL, real, reel, reef, BEEF

Flock of Fs (page 22)

1. fan; 2. fedora; 3. feet; 4. finger bowl;
5. fingers; 6. flying saucer; 7. football field;
8. frankfurter; 9. frog

Spin the Dials (page 23)

The word is POCKET.

Trees in Words (page 23)

1. teak; 2. yew; 3. elm; 4. elder; 5. pine; 6. ash;
7. fir

Number Climber (page 24)

Layer by Layer (page 25)

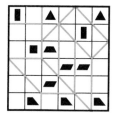

Geometric Shapes (page 25)

Name Calling (page 26)
1. moral; 2. virtue; 3. giraffe; 4. travel; 5. stronger

Rhyme Time (page 26)
1. got hot; 2. Cub snub; 3. slow flow; 4. dorm form; 5. rift shift; 6. reach beach; 7. regal eagle; 8. finer liner; 9. muddy study; 10. stock shock

Count the Dots (page 27)
100 dots

Ho-Hum Advice (page 27)
"When in doubt, sing loud."
—Robert Merrill

Let's Get Away From It All (pages 28–29)

Rock Around the Record Maze (page 30)

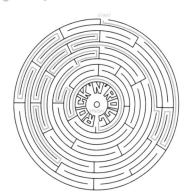

It Has a Ring (page 31)

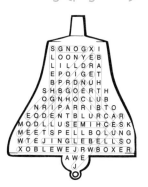

Answers

Sudoku (page 32)

2	3	8	1	9	7	6	4	5
4	9	5	2	6	3	7	1	8
1	7	6	5	4	8	3	2	9
8	2	7	6	1	5	9	3	4
5	1	4	3	8	9	2	6	7
9	6	3	4	7	2	8	5	1
6	4	9	8	2	1	5	7	3
7	5	2	9	3	4	1	8	6
3	8	1	7	5	6	4	9	2

Initial Impression (page 32)

1. Baltimore & Ohio
2. Cooperative for American Relief Everywhere
3. electrocardiogram (or -graph)
4. Greenwich Mean Time
5. International Standard Book Number
6. light-emitting diode
7. National Aeronautics and Space Administration
8. répondez, s'il vous plaît
9. surface-to-air missile
10. sealed with a kiss

Pathway (page 33)

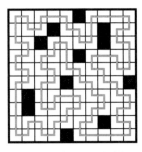

Donut Maze (page 34)

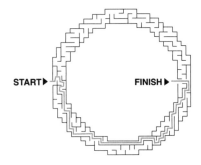

Time Will Tell (page 34)

wait and see

Geometric Shapes (page 35)

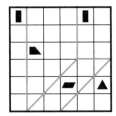

Cities and States (page 35)

Fargo; Indiana; Maine; Salem; Seattle; Texas

Traffic Light (pages 36–37)

Buy It Online (page 38)

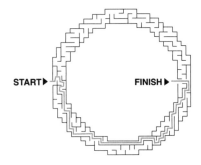

Rhyme Time (page 39)

1. see me; 2. top cop; 3. fat bat; 4. chow now;
5. last cast or past cast; 6. mars czars; 7. wrong thong; 8. pony's cronies

Try a Little Love (page 39)

There is more than one possible answer.
HATE, date, dote, dove, LOVE
HATE, have, hive, live, LOVE
HATE, late, lade, lode, LOVE

A Little Mix-up (page 40)

1. D: FIREWORKS; 2. F: KALEIDOSCOPE;
3. C: AIRPLANE; 4. A: CRAYONS;
5. E: GYROSCOPE; 6. B: POPSICLE

No Shoes, No Shirt, No Service (page 41)

12. Of the people turned away, 3 wore only socks, 1 wore only shoes, and 4 wore both.

Layer by Layer (page 41)

4			
3	5	6	7
2	9	8	
1	10		12
		11	

Dog Dishes (page 42)

All 3 dog dishes are the same size, so the 3 dogs must be the same size.

Bevy of Bs (page 43)

1. band shell; 2. banjo; 3. baseball bat; 4. baseball cap; 5. bench; 6. bicycle; 7. boat; 8. book; 9. boy; 10. branches; 11. bushes

Totally Cube-ular! (page 44)

A and B

The Ten Spot (page 45)

16: Ted TENnyson the Third of TEN atTENded a TENt dance with fifteen TENse gents preTENding to entertain nineteen TENder lasses with short atTENtion spans. In a TENder momenT, ENthralled by the music, TENnyson asked the DJ to play the hits of TEN Years After. TENnyson and his pal PaT ENdured eighT ENtire songs before a spaT ENded the night.

Shooting Star (page 45)

SLING

I Owe, I Owe... (page 46)

WORK, cork/wore, core, care, case, CASH

Name Calling (page 46)

1. separately; 2. ain't; 3. his home; 4. dimensions

And a 1, and a 2... (page 47)

				20	
8	4	4	3	1	20
3	2	6	7	7	25
9	8	1	1	6	25
8	9	9	2	5	33
2	3	1	3	8	17
30	26	21	16	27	21

Pretty Fontsy! (page 47)

m r h (X) t o d e G w L c ß
H J f i n Q m a z o z m V
e L o r k u F y w k P g
N D W v x t a T u (X) c
y b H v R k g l e j E t p U

Spinning Gray into Gold (page 48)

Your answers may vary.
1. GRAY, bray, brat, boat, goat, goad, GOLD
2. BLUE, flue, flux, flax, flay, fray, GRAY
3. BLACK, blank, bland, blend, bleed, breed, greed, GREEN
4. ROSE, rode, mode, made, JADE
5. TEAL, tell, till, tile, time, LIME

Number Theory (page 48)

There are three kinds of people—those who can count and those who can't.

Answers

The State of Things (page 49)

In the Drink (pages 50–51)

L	A	P	S	E	D		B	U	S	T		S	R	O
A	R	O	U	S	E		O	T	T	O		T	A	N
S	P	R	I	T	E		B	E	E	R	B	O	H	M
H	A	T	T	E	R	A	S		A	T	E	A	S	E
		O	E	R		S	L	I	D	E	R			
A	R	F	S		P	I	E	T	Y		A	B	B	E
S	E	C		P	A	N	D	A		S	T	R	U	M
F	E	A	R	E	D			P	L	E	A	S	E	
A	S	L	O	W		D	I	A	R	Y		N	E	R
R	E	L	Y		S	I	N	C	E		E	D	D	Y
		A	R	T	I	S	T		E	L	Y			
T	I	L	L	E	R		P	I	L	L	O	W	E	D
W	R	Y	S	M	I	L	E		A	L	P	I	N	E
I	A	N		E	P	I	C		T	I	E	N	D	A
T	E	N		T	E	S	T		H	E	R	E	O	N

Legion of Ls (page 52)
1. lady; 2. lamp post; 3. layer cake; 4. leaves; 5. lemon; 6. lemonade; 7. life jacket; 8. light; 9. lightbulb; 10. links; 11. lion; 12. loafers

Family Ties (page 53)
1. aunt; 2. cousin; 3. father; 4. mom; 5. mother; 6. niece; 7. papa; 8. parent; 9. sister; 10. son

Sudoku (page 53)

5	1	9	8	7	4	3	2	6
3	4	2	9	1	6	7	8	5
7	6	8	3	2	5	1	9	4
8	9	1	6	5	2	4	3	7
6	2	3	4	9	7	8	5	1
4	5	7	1	3	8	9	6	2
2	3	4	7	6	9	5	1	8
1	8	5	2	4	3	6	7	9
9	7	6	5	8	1	2	4	3

Countdown (page 54)

"When angry, count ten before you speak; if very angry, an hundred."
—Thomas Jefferson

"When angry, count four; when very angry, swear."
—Mark Twain

Job Search (page 54)
1. actor; 2. artist; 3. farmer; 4. maid; 5. mason; 6. model; 7. sailor; 8. tailor; 9. valet; 10. waiter; 11. warder; 12. writer

ABCD (page 55)

	A	3	0	2	0	2	2
	B	1	2	0	2	2	2
	C	1	2	2	2	1	1
A B C D		1	2	2	2	1	1
0 2 2 2		B	D	C	D	B	C
3 0 2 1		A	C	A	C	A	D
0 3 0 3		D	B	D	B	D	B
2 0 2 2		A	D	C	D	C	A
1 3 1 1		C	B	D	B	A	B
3 1 2 0		A	C	A	C	B	A

Rhyme Time (page 55)
1. big pig; 2. buy pie; 3. seek peak; 4. shrill drill; 5. scare bear; 6. mail trail; 7. mean queen; 8. chilly filly; 9. cheese please; 10. bigger rigger

Reach the "Sum"mit (page 56)

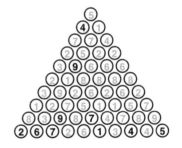

Funny Farm (page 58)
1. flying fish; 2. rooster laying egg; 3. alligator near barn; 4. giant pig; 5. mixed-up directions on weather vane; 6. unicorn; 7. bull being milked

The Times Tables are Turned! (page 59)

			75
2	3	5	30
4	5	4	80
3	1	2	6
24	15	40	20

Picnic Puzzle (page 59)

No; It's impossible to cover the remaining table-cloth squares with the hoagies. Draw an 8×8 checkerboard with alternating red-and-white squares. When you draw a pitcher of lemonade covering the diagonal corners, you will be covering either 2 red or 2 white squares (let's say red). When you put a hoagie on the table, it must cover a red and a white square. But there are now 32 white squares and only 30 red ones. Sally won't be able to do it.

Training Exercise (page 60)

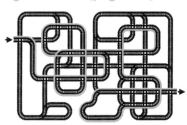

It's a Song (page 60)

"Bad Moon Rising" (1969 song by Creedence Clearwater Revival)

Count the Dots (page 61)

75 dots

Sound of Music (page 61)

The missing letter is S, as in "so." The sequence: do re mi fa so la ti do.

Sudoku (page 62)

6	4	1	5	3	8	9	2	7
7	8	3	2	9	4	5	6	1
2	9	5	1	7	6	4	8	3
5	6	7	9	4	3	8	1	2
3	1	4	8	2	7	6	9	5
9	2	8	6	5	1	7	3	4
1	5	2	4	8	9	3	7	6
4	7	9	3	6	2	1	5	8
8	3	6	7	1	5	2	4	9

East to West (page 62)

Your answers may vary.

1. EAST, vast, vest, WEST
2. BALL, bale/gall, gale, GAME
3. DOGS, does, woes, woos, WOOF
4. RAGS, rage, race, rice, RICH
5. WILD, wile, tile, tale, TAME
6. NAIL, fail, fall, fill, FILE
7. CATS, cots, dots, DOGS

Coffee Break (page 63)

Get a Move On (pages 64–65)

T	O	O	T		E	C	H	O		S	E	D	A	N
E	A	V	E		C	H	U	M		L	L	A	N	O
C	H	E	R		R	O	L	E		O	I	L	E	D
H	U	R	R	Y	U	P	A	N	D	W	A	I	T	
	C	A	R				S	O	P					
A	S	A		S	T	O	A		C	O	M	B	A	T
S	T	L	O		O	R	C	A		K	E	E	N	E
F	O	L	L	O	W	T	H	E	L	E	A	D	E	R
A	P	E	A	R		S	E	R	E		T	W	A	S
R	E	D	F	I	N		S	O	T	S		A	R	E
			G	O	O				A	P	R			
	B	E	H	I	N	D	T	H	E	T	I	M	E	S
O	L	E	A	N		E	R	A	S		N	E	R	O
D	E	L	T	A		T	I	L	T		T	R	A	Y
E	D	S	E	L		S	O	L	E		A	S	T	A

Answers

Count the Shapes (page 66)
There are 14 triangles.

Word Jigsaw (page 67)

How Many? (page 68)
1. dozen; 2. eight; 3. eighty; 4. eleven; 5. nine; 6. ninety; 7. one; 8. score; 9. seven; 10. seventy; 11. ten; 12. three; 13. twelve; 14. twenty; 15. zero

Three-Letter Anagrams (page 68)
1. won, now; 2. tap, pat; 3. tea, ate; 4. car, arc; 5. ewe, wee

ABCD (page 69)

				A	1	2	1	3	0	2
				B	2	2	2	0	2	1
				C	3	0	1	2	2	1
A	B	C	D	0	2	2	1	2	2
3	1	1	1	A	B	A	C	D	A
2	0	2	2	C	A	D	A	C	**D**
0	3	1	2	B	D	B	D	B	C
3	0	2	1	C	A	D	A	C	A
0	3	1	2	B	D	B	C	B	D
1	2	2	1	C	B	C	A	**D**	B

Prvrbs (page 69)
A stitch in time saves nine.
Better late than never.
All's well that ends well.

A Single Letter (page 70)
P

It's All Relative (page 70)
"When a man sits with a pretty girl for an hour, it seems like a minute. But let him sit on a hot stove for a minute—and it's longer than an hour. That's relativity."
—Albert Einstein

Dawn to Dusk (page 71)
Your answers may vary.
1. DAWN, darn, dark, dank, dunk, DUSK
2. JUMP, lump, lamp, lame, lane, LAND
3. BOOT, book, took, tock, tick, KICK
4. BOAT, moat, most, mist, fist, FISH
5. WAVE, wove, wore, sore, sure, SURF
6. KISS, miss, moss, loss, lose, LOVE

Related Women (page 71)
Mary is Sally's daughter.

Sudoku (page 72)

2	6	8	3	5	9	4	1	7
4	3	5	1	6	7	9	2	8
7	1	9	8	4	2	5	3	6
6	9	2	7	8	1	3	5	4
8	5	1	4	2	3	6	7	9
3	7	4	6	9	5	2	8	1
5	4	3	9	1	8	7	6	2
1	2	6	5	7	4	8	9	3
9	8	7	2	3	6	1	4	5

Making Music (page 72)
download songs

The But-Not Game (page 73)
Carol likes words with alternating consonants and vowels.

Game Time (page 73)
seventh-inning stretch

Tessellated Floor (page 74)

What's Missing? (page 75)
C: Catch as catch can

Three Ways (page 75)
C

Cruising Along (page 76)

```
S K C A N S E S S A L C K Y T
K C A C T I V I T I E S A H H
N E P R O M E N A D E W R C S
I D T M X G E S E M A G A N T
R R A A Z O N S H G N B O U E
D A I S S I N I R I Z A K L F
Y W N S B T I I B U G C E O U
R E W A W S F M S O N H Y O U
A T C G L F I I Y A I E T P B
R S M E A L S Z G G C F G E S
B D S T C R O L E S N U O C A
I S S K M O O R E T A T S Y U
L E C T U R E S V I D E O S N
L O U N G E S O L A R I U M A
R E T A E H T O U R S A L O N
```

900 Total (page 77)

The first column must contain the digits 1, 2, and 4 in some order. There are many combinations.

Here are two:

```
  138     153
  265     268
+497     +479
  900     900
```

For Your Eyes Only (page 77)

All 4 stars are the same size.

High Times (pages 78–79)

```
B E T A   P O W E R   S T A G
I C O N   A B A C I   P I M A
T H E T O W E R O F B A B E L
S O R E N E S S   L A R I N E
      D A R E   R E R E A D S
S C R A G S   D U M B
E L A T E   G I N A   W A N
T O W E R I N G I N F E R N O
S T S   C A I N   A M A T I
      V E S T   S U P P E R
W A S P I S H   R I C E
A C K A C K   G E N E R A T E
T H E L E A N I N G T O W E R
T O I L   T A S T E   R A N I
S O N S   E N T E R   S Y N E
```

Mrs. Smith's Daughters (page 80)

The youngest child is not Sarah (Clue 1), Jane, or Anna (Clue 2), so it is Kate. The oldest child is not Jane or Anna (Clue 2), so it is Sarah. Two girls are older than Anna (Clue 4), so she is 2 and Jane is 3. Jane is the blond (Clue 4), so her eyes are brown and Anna's hair is brown (Clue 2). Sarah does not have black hair (Clue 1), so Kate does, and Sarah is the redhead whose eyes are green (Clue 4). Kate does not have hazel eyes (Clue 3), so her eyes are blue and 2-year-old, brown-haired Anna has hazel eyes.

In summary:

Age	Name	Hair	Eyes
4	Sarah	red	green
3	Jane	blond	brown
2	Anna	brown	hazel
1	Kate	black	blue

Remember Me? (pages 81–82)

UMBRELLA, FLAG, GRATER, DOUGH-NUTS, HARMONICA, ANCHOR, PINEAPPLE, COMPASS

Amazing Bout with a Trout (page 83)

Cryptoquote (page 83)

"Put all your eggs in one basket—and watch that basket."
—Mark Twain

Crowd of Cs (page 84)

1. calendar; 2. candle; 3. canopy; 4. cap; 5. car; 6. carpet; 7. chest of drawers; 8. clock; 9. corn; 10. counterpane; 11. covers; 12. cup; 13. curtains

Sweet Dreams (page 84)

SLEEP, bleep, bleed, breed, bread, dread, DREAM

Answers

Sudoku (page 85)

4	6	1	9	3	2	7	8	5
8	7	2	5	4	1	3	9	6
9	5	3	8	6	7	4	2	1
2	1	5	7	8	4	6	3	9
7	4	6	3	2	9	1	5	8
3	9	8	1	5	6	2	4	7
5	8	7	4	1	3	9	6	2
1	2	4	6	9	8	5	7	3
6	3	9	2	7	5	8	1	4

Bird Wisdom (page 85)

1. A bird in hand is worth two in the bush.
2. Birds of a feather flock together.
3. The early bird gets the worm.

Altered States (page 86)

Theme: Each word or phrase is an anagram of a U.S. state.

Rhyme Time (page 87)

1. more ore; 2. mean dean; 3. tall mall;
4. seek leak; 5. core chore; 6. gray beret;
7. mummy rummy; 8. deeper sleeper;
9. cheaper keeper; 10. last broadcast

Triangle Cut (page 87)

ABCD (page 88)

A	2	2	1	1	1	2
B	2	0	2	2	2	1
C	2	1	1	0	3	2
A B C D	0	3	2	3	0	1

2	1	1	2	A	D	B	D	C	A
2	1	2	1	C	A	D	B	A	C
1	2	2	1	B	D	C	A	C	B
1	2	2	1	C	A	B	D	B	C
2	1	2	1	A	C	D	B	C	A
1	2	0	3	B	D	A	D	B	D

Two Rules (page 88)

There are two rules for ultimate success in life: Never tell everything you know.

Corporate Office Maze (page 89)

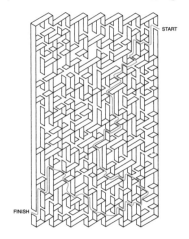

Cube It! (page 90)

3	4	3	
4	7	7	
	7	3	6
	4	7	3

Count the Shapes (page 90)

There are 22 rectangles.

Myriad of Ms (page 91)

1. mackintosh; 2. maid; 3. mallet; 4. man;
5. mask; 6. medal; 7. meteor; 8. mice;
9. microphone; 10. microphone stand; 11. moon;
12. moose; 13. mop; 14. mountain

Star (page 91)

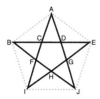

The new triangles are: A-B-C, A-D-E, B-F-I,
H-I-J, E-G-J, A-B-J, A-E-I, B-E-J, A-I-J, B-E-I,
A-C-E, D-E-J, G-I-J, B-H-I, A-B-F, A-B-D,
B-C-I, F-I-J, E-H-J, A-E-G, A-B-E, A-E-J,
E-I-J, B-I-J, A-B-I.

Treed (pages 92–93)

A-Dissection (page 94)

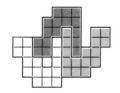

Card Positions (page 94)

left to right: king of hearts, jack of diamonds,
queen of spades, ace of clubs

Turnabout Maze (page 95)

Count the Dots (page 96)

93 dots

Chess Squares (page 96)

There are 204 squares in all:
1 × 1 squares = 64
2 × 2 squares = 49
3 × 3 squares = 36
4 × 4 squares = 25
5 × 5 squares = 16
6 × 6 squares = 9
7 × 7 squares = 4
8 × 8 square = 1

Sudoku (page 97)

7	4	1	3	2	5	9	8	6
8	2	3	9	6	7	4	5	1
9	6	5	4	8	1	3	7	2
4	9	2	6	7	3	8	1	5
5	8	6	2	1	4	7	3	9
3	1	7	5	9	8	6	2	4
2	3	8	1	4	6	5	9	7
6	5	9	7	3	2	1	4	8
1	7	4	8	5	9	2	6	3

Four-Letter Anagrams (page 97)

1. odor, door; 2. lids, slid; 3. runt, turn;
4. part, rapt; 5. ring, grin; 6. lamp, palm;
7. form, from; 8. pace, cape

Problematic Pool Hall (page 98)

1. neither lamp is directly over a table; 2. pool
cue is through the ball; 3. bent cue; 4. right side

Answers

leg of table is too tall; 5. waiting player's left foot is backward; 6. egg frying on table; 7. waiting player has 6 fingers on right hand; 8. all the balls are white (no numbers)

Four Square (page 98)

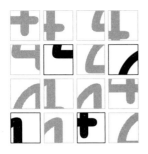

Decorative Word Search (page 100)

What a Whistle (pages 101–102)

1. Connecticut
2. b) American kestrel
3. 14
4. False
5. c) raw meat
6. a) a bad wing
7. b) falcon
8. b) retrained it to fly
9. a) a certain whistle
10. b) a screech owl

Times Square (page 103)

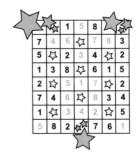

5	1	5	5	125
1	7	7	7	343
6	6	1	6	216
2	2	5	1	20
60	84	175	210	

Star Power (page 103)

Sister's Brothers (page 104)

Diane has 3 brothers.

Winter Evening (page 104)

1. snake coming out of birdcage; 2. woman sitting on giant rabbit; 3. woman holding shovel; 4. tie hanging outside of portrait; 5. cat coming out of wall; 6. chair floating near wall; 7. hand in fire

Fold-O-Rama Maze (page 105)

Starboard Course Maze (page 106)

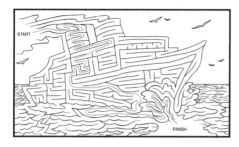

Alphabet Fill-In (page 106)

1. SOLID; 2. BAYOU; 3. RELAX; 4. ZILCH;
5. KHAKI; 6. VENOM; 7. JUNTA; 8. QUERY

Name That Nickname (page 107)

The man nicknamed Tubba is 44. He drives a
station wagon, is a beer-bottle capper, and roots
for the Raiders.

Four Sisters (page 108)

Robert is not married to Roberta (Clue 1),
Paula (Clue 2), or Alberta (Clue 3), so his wife
is Carla. Albert is not married to Alberta (Clue
1) or Roberta (Clue 3), so his wife is Paula. Paul
is not married to Roberta (Clue 2), so his wife is
Alberta. Therefore, Carl's wife must be Roberta,
whose last name is not Carlson or Robertson
(Clue 1) or Paulson (Clue 4); it is Albertson.
Robert and Carla's last name is not Robertson or
Carlson (Clue 1), so it is Paulson. Since Robert
Paulson is not the man in the second half of Clue
3, Albert and Paula's last name is Robertson.
This leaves Carlson as the last name of Paul and
Alberta.

In summary:

Alberta	Paul	Carlson
Carla	Robert	Paulson
Paula	Albert	Robertson
Roberta	Carl	Albertson

Number Crossword (page 109)

Bookend Letters (page 109)

DANGLED; ECLIPSE; PRIMP; STRAITS

Sevens (pages 110-111)

It's White (page 112)

Word Square and Memory Check (pages 113-114)

ADIEU, STORY, HUSSY, RINSO, MAMAS,
APSES

Our Loopy Lingo (page 115)

If you have a bunch of odds and ends and get rid
of all but one of them, what do you have?

183

Answers

Four Squares to Three (page 115)

Deluge of Ds (page 116)

1. dagger; 2. derby (hat); 3. desk/dresser;
4. digital clock; 5. digits; 6. dinosaur; 7. dish;
8. dog; 9. dollar; 10. door; 11. doorknob;
12. doughnuts; 13. drapes; 14. drawer

Bundle Up! (page 116)

SCARF, scare, stare, stave, slave, clave, clove,
GLOVE

Pretzel Logic (page 117)

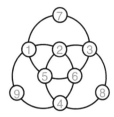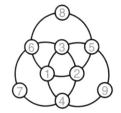

How Many Rectangles? (page 117)

There are 34 rectangles in all: 2 rectangles are
4×2; 4 rectangles are 3×2; 4 rectangles are 4×1;
16 rectangles are 2×1, and 8 rectangles are 3×1.

Jelly Bean Jar Maze (page 118)

Sudoku (page 119)

3	2	5	7	1	6	4	8	9
1	9	6	5	4	8	7	2	3
4	7	8	9	2	3	1	6	5
8	3	2	4	6	9	5	7	1
6	1	7	8	3	5	9	4	2
5	4	9	1	7	2	6	3	8
2	5	4	6	8	1	3	9	7
9	6	3	2	5	7	8	1	4
7	8	1	3	9	4	2	5	6

Fresh to Stale (page 119)

Your answers may vary.
1. FRESH, flesh, flash, slash, slosh, sloth, slots,
slats, stats, state, STALE
2. STICK, stack, stark, stare, store, STONE
3. LOSE, lone, line, fine, FIND

Perfect Square (page 120)

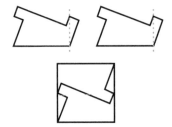

For Your Eyes Only (page 120)

All 4 arrows are the same length.

Rhyme Time (page 121)

1. meek eek; 2. drab crab; 3. need speed; 4. buff
enough; 5. couth youth 6. hound sound; 7. sharp
escarp; 8. devout scout; 9. tourist list; 10. crabby
cabbie; 11. flabby tabby; 12. sublime crime;
13. exalted malted; 14. cheaper sweeper;
15. grandstand band; 16. tourney journey

Executive Disorder (pages 122–123)

There are only 37 presidents' names on the list, because Adams, Bush, Harrison, Johnson, and Roosevelt were each the names of 2 different presidents, and because Grover Cleveland served as both the 22nd and 24th president.

Sock Drawer (page 124)

Tom would have to pull out 3 socks. Because there are only 2 different colors, if he pulls out three, at least two—and maybe all three—will be the same color.

Horde of Hs (page 124)

1. hairbrush; 2. hammock; 3. hand; 4. hand mirror; 5. hangers; 6. harp; 7. hat; 8. hay; 9. heart; 10. hem; 11. hockey stick; 12. horn; 13. horse; 14. horseshoe

Decorating Dilemma (page 125)

The daughter doesn't want wallpaper (paragraph 2), paneling (par. 2), or Day-Glo paint (par. 1), so she must want the checkerboard-carpeted wall and be named Lee (par. 1), and she is the upstairs resident (par. 3). Dale doesn't want wallpaper (par. 2) or paneling (par. 2), so Dale wants Day-Glo paint. Since the son wants Day-Glo paint (par. 1), Dale must be the son. His bedroom is either next door or in the converted garage. Pat,

writing the letter, by several references is the father, and he wants paneling (par. 2). This leaves Leslie to be the mom, who wants wallpaper. In paragraph 3, he refers to "an occupant" of the next room, which implies a husband and wife, making the son the resident of the converted garage.

In summary:

Dale	Son	Day-Glo paint	Converted garage
Lee	Daughter	B&W carpet	Upstairs room
Leslie	Mom	Wallpaper	Room next door
Pat	Dad	Paneling	Room next door

Word Jigsaw (page 126)

ABCD (page 127)

```
  A 0 1 3 1 2 2
  B 2 2 0 2 1 2
  C 2 2 0 3 0 2
A B C D 2 1 3 0 3 0
2 1 2 1 C B A C D A
1 3 1 1 B C D B A B
1 1 3 1 C B A C D C
2 2 0 2 D A D B A B
1 2 2 1 B D A C B C
2 0 1 3 D C D A D A
```

Geometric Shapes (page 127)

Answers

Layer by Layer (page 128)

```
12  13 14    17
  11 10   15
           16
   1      9
       5  8
   2
   3   4     7
              6
```

You Said It! (page 128)

1. No one seems to know for sure what people want these days, except that they won't accept a penny less.
2. Today's travelers have proven that the world is certainly round. It is their wallets that are flat.

Shoot-out at the K.O. Corral (page 130)

1. outlaw is wearing two hats; 2. outlaw is wearing a blindfold; 3. pistol finger; 4. banana gun; 5. outlaw is wearing a sheriff badge; 6. the jack-in-the-box has hands up; 7. hands through the roof of the stagecoach; 8. gas tank on coach; 9. shooter in coach is out-of-perspective; 10. steering wheel on stagecoach; 11. airplane soaring overhead

Sudoku (page 131)

9	1	3	2	5	6	4	7	8
4	5	6	9	8	7	1	2	3
8	2	7	4	1	3	9	6	5
7	3	5	1	9	4	6	8	2
2	8	1	7	6	5	3	4	9
6	4	9	8	3	2	7	5	1
3	6	4	5	2	9	8	1	7
5	9	8	6	7	1	2	3	4
1	7	2	3	4	8	5	9	6

Ideal Advice (page 131)

"And so, my fellow Americans, ask not what your country can do for you; ask what you can do for your country."
—John F. Kennedy

Animal House (pages 132–133)

Entourage of Es (page 134)

1. earmuffs; 2. egg; 3. egg cup; 4. eggplant; 5. eight; 6. elbows; 7. elephant; 8. elephant ear; 9. elevator; 10. embroidery; 11. embroidery hoop; 12. end table; 13. English muffin; 14. evening gown

Weird Word Search (pages 135–136)

GHOSTLY, UNCANNY, CHILLING, BIZARRE, STRANGE, FREAKY, ARCANE, MACABRE

Geometric Shapes (page 137)

Letter Lesson (page 137)

"Now, in English, the letter which most frequently occurs is E. Afterward, the succession runs thus: A, O, I, D, H, N, R, S, T, U, Y, C, F, G, L, M, W, B, K, P, Q, X, Z. E predominates so remarkably, that an individual sentence of any length is rarely seen, in which it is not the prevailing character."
—Edgar Allan Poe

Odd-Even Logidoku (page 138)

3	9	5	4	1	2	8	7	6
6	4	1	7	3	8	9	2	5
8	7	2	5	6	9	4	3	1
4	3	8	6	2	7	1	5	9
1	6	9	3	5	4	2	8	7
2	5	7	8	9	1	3	6	4
5	8	3	9	4	6	7	1	2
7	1	4	2	8	5	6	9	3
9	2	6	1	7	3	5	4	8

Layer by Layer (page 138)

2				
		3	4	5
1				
		10	6	
11				7
12	9		8	

Charmer Maze (page 139)

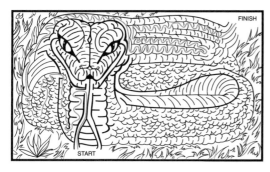

Bookend Letters (page 139)

1. YEARLY; 2. DELUDED; 3. REVOLVER; 4. SEATS; 5. LEVEL; 6. NEURON

The Morning Landscape (page 140)

Sean's first stop was at the Browns', and on his second stop he planted the maple tree (Clue 3). Both of these addresses had to be Lanes (Clue 3), but the maple tree could not be planted on Maple Lane (Clue 2), so it was planted on Apple Lane, and the Browns lived on Maple Lane. The pear tree was planted at his third stop, and the Whites' house was his last stop of the morning (Clue 4). The pear tree was not planted on Pear Drive, so it was planted on Elm Drive. Pear Drive was the address of Sean's last stop (the Whites' house), where he planted a fruit tree (Clue 2), the apple tree. This leaves the elm tree to be planted at his first stop, the Browns' house on Maple Lane. Finally, since the Greys did not live on Apple Lane (Clue 1), they lived on Elm Drive, and the Greens had a maple tree planted in their yard on Apple Lane.

In summary:

First	Elm tree	Browns	Maple Lane
Second	Maple tree	Greens	Apple Lane
Third	Pear tree	Greys	Elm Drive
Fourth	Apple tree	Whites	Pear Drive

Shakespeare's Women (page 141)

L	A	R	T	A	P	O	E	L	C	L	S	R	M	L
J	U	L	I	E	T	G	A	C	E	D	O	I	A	E
U	T	C	E	T	A	C	E	H	E	N	Y	D	R	L
N	N	E	E	P	E	R	C	Y	A	R	Y	R	I	I
O	P	H	E	L	I	A	O	E	N	M	E	O	N	Z
R	S	N	N	H	M	T	L	L	A	C	H	S	A	A
C	N	A	E	O	S	E	E	C	I	R	T	A	E	B
A	U	D	R	E	Y	R	B	L	R	R	N	L	U	E
S	D	D	I	I	A	E	A	A	A	O	E	I	I	T
S	N	I	S	A	T	I	I	E	M	M	E	N	M	H
A	N	S	S	H	N	L	L	E	T	B	M	E	O	E
N	A	A	A	S	U	A	D	E	R	L	I	L	G	G
D	O	B	G	J	E	S	S	I	C	A	L	A	E	N
R	J	E	D	E	E	R	H	E	R	M	I	O	N	E
A	I	L	E	D	R	O	C	M	I	R	A	N	D	A

Leftover letters spell:
LADY NORTHUMBERLAND

Wise Words (page 142)

1 Most of us are loyal—when we reach a certain age, we like to stick to it.
2. The things most people want to know are none of their business.

Answers

3. Nothing is impossible to the man who doesn't have to do it himself.

4. Thinking well is wise; planning well is wiser; doing well is wisest and best of all.

5. You can keep your head above water if you hold your chin up.

Kingdom of Ks (page 143)

1. kangaroo; 2. kayak; 3. kerchief; 4. keystone; 5. kite; 6. knapsack; 7. knife; 8. knitting; 9. knitting needles; 10. knot

Mister Ed-ucation (pages 144-145)

Straight Line Challenge (page 146)

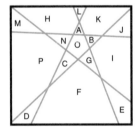

Plant Life (page 146)

1. bark; 2. bush; 3. fern; 4. flower; 5. foliage; 6. leaf; 7. petal; 8. shrub; 9. stalk; 10. stem

It's a Shore Thing (pages 147-148)

1. flying disc; 2. conch shell; 3. Goop; 4. stripes; 5. crocodile; 6. Breeze; 7. lobster; 8. shorts, jacket, hat; 9. megaphone; 10. four

A Bright Idea (page 148)

He flipped a switch and filled the room with light.

Numerical Word Search (page 149)

Six-String Maze (page 150)

Swarm of Ss (page 151)

1. sails; 2. salami (or sausage); 3. sandwich; 4. sash (window); 5. saucer; 6. shadows; 7. shell; 8. ship; 9. shoes (or sneakers); 10. sill; 11. sink; 12. slacks; 13. smile; 14. soap; 15. stool; 16. strings; 17. sun; 18. sweater; 19. sword

Word of Mouth (page 151)

1. eat; 2. gape; 3. grin; 4. lisp; 5. palate; 6. pout; 7. sing; 8. smile; 9. taste; 10. teeth; 11. tongue

Movie Weekend (page 152)

Sat. matinee: Western; Altman; Bijou
Sat. night: Comedy; Brooks; Plaza
Sun. matinee: Sci-fi; Allen; Odeon
Sun. night: Mystery; Truffaut; Jewel

Sudoku (page 153)

Hex Dissection (page 153)

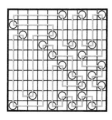

Sawtooth Cube (page 154)

A and C

Password Maker (pages 155–156)

COWBOY GOLDEN, FREEDOM ELEPHANT, QUOTATION ORANGE, FLUTTER CAMPUS, MOUNTAIN CYMBAL, ADVICE KETTLE, PIANO LOBSTER, PRESTIGE NINETEEN, BELIEF HAMMER, CONCEPT SALAMANDER

Alternate Corners (page 156)

Lost Weekend (pages 158–159)

Headline Howlers (page 160)

1. Kids make nutritious snacks. 2. Red tape holds up new bridges. 3. Astronaut takes blame for gas in spacecraft. 4. Plane too close to ground, crash probe told.

Geometric Shapes (page 160)

Fabulous Creatures (page 161)

1. c) UNICORN; 2. d) DRAGON;
3. f) MINOTAUR; 4. a) CENTAUR;
5. b) MERMAID; 6. e) GRIFFIN

Logidoku (page 162)

Answers

Layer by Layer (page 162)

Forget-Me-Not and Friends (pages 163–164)

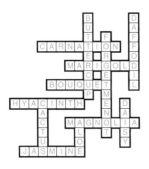

MAGNOLIA, BUTTERCUP, JASMINE, DAFFODIL, DAISY, FORGET-ME-NOT, CARNATION, ALOE

Made of Money (page 165)

Leftover letters spell: THE LOVE OF MONEY IS THE ROOT OF ALL EVIL

As You Will (pages 166–167)

Sudoku (page 168)

9	6	5	3	4	8	7	1	2
8	4	2	7	6	1	5	3	9
1	7	3	5	9	2	6	8	4
4	5	1	2	3	9	8	7	6
3	2	9	8	7	6	4	5	1
7	8	6	4	1	5	2	9	3
2	3	4	1	8	7	9	6	5
5	9	8	6	2	3	1	4	7
6	1	7	9	5	4	3	2	8

A Gourmet Guide to Toad Egos (page 168)

Rattling his pots and pans, Thomas Trencherman, master chef, addressed his class. "Snap to, my foodies, time for breakfast! For a snack with coffee, let's have some delicious DANISH PASTRIES. Now we'll go through an entire dinner menu, from APPETIZER to DESSERT. Let's start with a bowl of SOUP DU JOUR, which today is CLAM CHOWDER, then offer a chilled SHRIMP COCKTAIL. Entrée choices will include SURF AND TURF, consisting of medium-rare NEW YORK STRIP, served with a steaming hot LOBSTER TAIL. For dessert, a choice of TIRAMISU or the ever-popular CRÈME BRÛLÉE. BON APPÉTIT to you!"

INDEX

continued on page 192